GOD OF ALL COMFORT

40 DAYS
TO A
Calmer Spirit

DaySpring

LIVE YOUR FAITH

Contents

Dear Friends,

I'm inviting you on a 40-day journey to discover more about who you are, how infinitely and intimately loved you are, and what that means in your day-to-day life.

When life brings uncertainty and discomfort, as difficult as it can be, we are also given abundant opportunities to grow on our spiritual paths. Many of us discover in those times that we have just as much to unlearn as we have to learn—just as much to let go of as we have to receive. And at some point, we realize there is so much more to us than we've ever known, and that understanding and embracing our God-created selves is the wonderful work of a lifetime.

As you read each entry in this book, answer the questions honestly, and consider the suggestions that follow, I pray you will find your load lightened and your heart lifted. I hope you'll discover more about what weighs you down and holds you back and that you'll be inspired to move forward with greater awareness, freedom, and authenticity.

Go at the pace you need; make this journey your own. But make the promise to yourself that you'll complete it. Because you are worth every moment you invest in creating this beautiful life God is calling you to live each day.

Snuggle in God's arms . . .
let Him cradle you,
comfort you, reassure you
of His all-sufficient
power and love.

KAY ARTHUR

The Source of True Comfort

Comfort comes to us in many forms, and we all have unique ways of experiencing it. We may feel the need for it more at certain times in our lives than at other times. But one thing is certain for every person seeking solace today: it is found most deeply in the very real presence of God. There are no requirements for receiving the divine rest and reassurance He offers. No boxes to check, no favor to earn, and no need to measure up. We simply accept the daily invitation to draw close to Him and hear His heart.

The truth is, no one knows what tomorrow holds—and that's okay. In fact, we're not meant to. There's something so much bigger going on than our human desire to control our circumstances and make life less challenging for ourselves. God is creating an infinitely greater picture—one that we can only see a tiny part of right now. And the more we understand and embody this truth, the more peace we will find in letting go and letting Him do His beautiful work within us.

You may have a specific reason for holding this book in your hands—maybe you chose it because you're walking through a tough season of life, or maybe someone who cares for you thought it would speak to your heart. No matter how these messages have reached you today, just remember—the truths they contain are timeless. They can be held in your heart for whenever you need them most to bring you comfort and encouragement in the days and years to come.

Reflect

Why did you open this book, and what are you hoping to receive from its pages?

_____

_____

When you think about living with a calmer spirit in your daily life,
what does that look like to you?

_____

_____

Can you recall a time when you experienced God's comforting presence when you needed it most?
Describe it here.

_____

_____

What is one verse from Scripture that brings peace and reassurance to your heart? Write it here.

_____

_____

What is one commitment you can make to yourself to help you finish the journey through these pages?

_____

_____

Respond

These messages are for you to read in your own way and at your own pace. They might speak to you differently today than they will tomorrow. And whenever you are ready, they are laid out for you in three parts:

Read: Each day, you'll read a reflection that invites you to experience God's comfort, reassurance, and guidance in a new way. It might be about something you're struggling with right now, or something you may walk through in the future, or even something someone you know is facing in their life. The thoughts and experiences shared here are universal. We all know how it feels to be stifled by fear and freed by faith—and everything that happens in between. This is a journey we can walk together, and the more support and encouragement we share, the better our journey will be.

Reflect: After reading the daily message, take a few moments to answer the questions that follow. You will likely discover some things you didn't know about yourself as you write them out. Sometimes we have more answers within us than we realize, but they just need the chance to be heard.

Respond: You can choose how to respond to the thoughts shared in these pages. There will be suggestions for actions that you can take to help bring the message into your daily life, but you're the one who knows how to make that happen. And most importantly, God may lead you to take action in unique and surprising ways as you hear Him speak to your heart.

Surrender to what is.
Let go of what was.
Have faith in what will be.

SONIA RICOTTI

Letting Go, Living Free

We all face situations in life that remind us that we aren't in control of anything, really, except our own thoughts and actions. Maybe it happens when we step onto an airplane that someone else is flying. Or when we've entrusted a sick loved one into the care of a hospital staff. Or when we're hoping for a certain outcome, and we just don't know which way it's going to go. Sometimes when there's a lot up in the air, the idea of micromanaging the universe seems quite appealing. Sure, we may trust God to take care of us, but we have some really specific ideas about how He might go about doing that!

It's okay that we have a hard time letting go of expectations. They are simply our best attempts to create the life we think will be best for us. And often, we're just trying to help ourselves feel safe in times of uncertainty. It can be tough to admit that those expectations are made of our very limited understanding of the big picture and of the way God is allowing our lives to unfold in His perfect way and time. But here's an encouraging thought: those up-in-the-air moments can be wonderful (not *easy*, but wonderful) catalysts for our spiritual growth. They are the moments that expand our capacity to trust—the "Be still, and know that I am God" moments (Psalm 46:10). The ones where we stop overthinking, overplanning, and overworking ourselves to try and make something happen. When we breathe deeply and remember: *All will be well because it's all in His hands.* Every last detail.

Reflect

Recall a recent time when you felt out of control. What was your natural reaction?

_____

_____

What negative thoughts do you struggle with when you face a situation that's not in your hands?

_____

_____

What are some of God's truths you can remind yourself of in those moments of uncertainty?

_____

_____

What are some everyday opportunities in which you can let go of control and trust in God's plan?

_____

_____

How can you remind yourself to trust God more often—maybe with a quote or verse hung up somewhere you can't miss it? Maybe a token you wear or carry with you every day?

_____

_____

Respond

Even when we aren't facing something epic and life-changing, we have little opportunities every day to practice letting go of control, and that builds our spiritual muscles for navigating the bigger things. Next time you're standing in line at a grocery store or coffee shop, frustrated by someone's slow progress, remind yourself that God's timing is perfect. There are reasons you're where you are in this time of your life. You can even look around for how God is working in this season of your life. Maybe the guy behind you needs a reassuring smile. Or the barista in front of you could use some extra grace at the moment. Guess what? You can be the one to offer it! You might be traveling and your rental car deal falls through or you miss your flight. Before scrambling to figure out your next move, stop yourself and take a soul-deep breath. Find reassurance in the truth that God already knew how this would play out and there was a reason He allowed it. Ask for guidance. Trust that He has something better for you down the line.

Sure, things may get uncomfortable before they start to make sense, but you already know the story will end well because it always ends with Him. That practice of surrender is one of the surest and shortest paths to peace that any of us can take. The more we experience the freedom that's found in letting go of our expectations, the more we will enjoy the journey—even the tough parts, because He often hides the silver linings there!

We must cultivate our own garden.

VOLTAIRE

Growing Good Thoughts

There's something our Creator has given us to care for, like a garden, and the more we tend to it, the more peace and assurance we will live with all day long. That "something" is our minds. And sometimes, these minds of ours are filled with good, true, and beautiful things. But other times, we can experience just the opposite. Let's call it the "snowball effect." Sound familiar? It happens when small worries or concerns are left unattended, start gaining ground, and grow bigger and bigger until they suddenly seem larger than life. Over time, those thoughts take up more and more precious space in our minds that could be filled instead with the good stuff like joy, gratitude, and contentment.

God gave us the potential to live with a vibrant inner landscape, and there are new things growing and blooming within us every day. But He also gave us the job of being caretakers of that landscape. Our minds can't thrive if we don't make the effort to nurture them, which means protecting them from what doesn't belong there and making sure we take in plenty that does. It takes intention and practice to create fertile ground for those life-giving, faith-filled thoughts to take root within us. If we wait until the weeds of doubt and fear have taken over, it may be a lot longer before we can feel deep inner peace again in any lasting way.

It helps to remind ourselves from time to time that we're in charge of these amazing minds we possess, even if it doesn't feel that way sometimes. *We* get to decide what stays and what goes when it comes to our thoughts, and that will set the tone for every day of our lives. So, how's it going for you in there?

Reflect

What kind of gardener are you when it comes to caring for your mind?

_____

_____

What weeds may be trying to grow among your thoughts lately?
What specific worries and fears tend to steal your daily joy?

_____

_____

Are there certain relationships, experiences, times of the year (or even the day)
that cause you to struggle more internally? Why do you think that is?

_____

_____

Can you think of some simple, intentional things you can do to help keep your mind
more peaceful and hopeful? Write them here.

_____

_____

What are a few verses that inspire you to lift your thoughts to God? Write them here.

_____

_____

Respond

As you've probably noticed, the Bible is full of inspiration about caring for our minds. God knows that whatever is inside us will always work its way out somehow. And if we want to live vibrant, Spirit-led lives, we must protect ourselves against thoughts that are constantly pulling us in the other direction.

See if you can get a picture of what's going on within your mind right now. Try asking yourself questions like these: How's life been feeling for me lately? Have I had an underlying sense of peace and trust in God's guidance, even amid my daily challenges? Or have I had a sense of foreboding, dread, or uncertainty in some way? Consider sitting quietly in prayer and asking for any "snowballs" to be revealed that might be causing anxiety and stealing your joy.

And here's something you can do that takes just a few minutes. Consider trying it once, and if it's helpful, you might decide to make it a regular practice: List any persistent thoughts or worries that you feel are weighing you down right now—even those small, nagging ones that just never seem to go away. If there are to-dos that keep calling for your attention, add them to the list too, and think of a few steps you might take toward resolving them. Make that call you've been putting off, gather some info—whatever small thing you can do to simplify and reduce stress for yourself. Then, acknowledge the things on your list that are out of your control and give them to God. Remember: it's all a process, but each small step you take can remove something negative and create more space within you for things that are positive, and that means greater freedom and joy in your life every day.

Never trade

your uniqueness

for approval.

JOY MARINO

Rocking the Boat

Our lives are filled with decisions that only we can make. Of course, a lot of those are small ones—what to wear, who to have coffee with, where to go for a haircut. But sometimes, they're bigger decisions—the kind we feel the need to seek God's guidance for. And as we do our best to follow His lead, we're invited to rest in the assurance that we're making the right decisions for us, regardless of the countless opinions of others.

This can be especially tough when we're feeling called to blaze a trail in some way—maybe being the first person in our family or inner circle to do something different. It might be a big move, or a new church, or even being honest about something no one else wants to address. There are many ways this can play out in our lives, and it's never easy to be the pioneer.

Often, people don't want to deal with someone in their circle of influence making a change. Maybe it brings up something for *them* that they don't want to look at. Maybe they're quite comfortable in their relationship with you, even though it's clear there are some things that need to be brought to light. Maybe watching you follow *your* dreams reminds them that they gave up on *theirs*. Imagine a mobile above a baby's crib. When you touch just one part, all the other parts naturally have to shift because they're connected. That's just how this human family works—and not everyone is thrilled about it!

Can you imagine what it was like for Jesus—all the people He disappointed and the earthly expectations He did not meet because He chose to listen to One Voice instead of many?

It shouldn't surprise us that we, too, may be called to rock the boat in our own way from time to time as we follow Him throughout our lives.

Reflect

Have you felt supported in following your own path or held back by others' expectations?
Explain below.

_____

_____

Can you describe a time when you were the one who had to step up and make a change,
even when it wasn't a popular decision?

_____

_____

Is there anything new that you feel God may be nudging you toward in your life right now?
If so, write about it below. And include whether you are excited or hesitant—or both?

_____

_____

How supportive are you when someone close to you starts making changes,
even if they involve adjustments for you to make?

_____

_____

Who in your life would you say has been the most supportive of you, and how?

_____

_____

Respond

Every day there are things for us to navigate—decisions, situations, relationships—and we will face them in one of two ways: in fear or in faith. If we put other people's opinions on a pedestal, if we compromise our calling to keep others comfortable, if we convince ourselves to turn back because it hurts too much to feel isolated or disapproved of, we're acting out of fear. And although God loves and accepts us just as much in our fear as in our faith, He wants more for us. He sees who we can become and how much more joy and purpose we can live with if we are able to trust in His guidance, no matter what others think.

Start noticing the times in your life when you feel swayed by the opinions and influence of others. Remind yourself that those are directions from someone else's compass. And while there may be great wisdom in their advice, you have the freedom and responsibility to discern God's leading for yourself. Don't ever forget that you have your *own* inner compass to guide you, provided by your Maker. When you find yourself wondering what to do next, you can always ask Him for direction first.

Making much-needed changes can take a lot of trust and courage. And even if you aren't facing a big transition right now, God promises His guidance for *every* step—not just the epic ones. When you're feeling a little lost, you can always dig into His Word and find reassurance in His promises to give you clear direction. Above all, grant yourself lots of grace. God does! He knows you're doing the best you can to take positive steps in your life, and that's a wonderful direction to be taking!

Let us pray every day
with hearts wide open
so that God might meet us
in whatever way He chooses.

ANONYMOUS

Connecting with God

Prayer is a lifelong conversation with God that's unique to each of us. And especially during tough times, we learn that prayer is so much deeper than an obligation; it can be a haven for our restless spirits, a refreshing place where we can be our truest selves in the presence of the purest love.

That's why it's good to remember that the way we pray will likely evolve throughout our lives as we are drawn to connect with God in new ways. And the more open we are to that change, the more authentic our relationship with Him will continue to be.

For example, there are times when we go to pray that we have to admit we just aren't feelin' it. Maybe we're stuck on the hamster wheel of overthinking, or we're tired or discouraged or even (if we're honest) unmotivated at the moment. We know how much we need that sacred connection with God, so we show up hoping that something will click. Yesterday or last week may have been completely different. That's just how it works! Our spiritual connections ebb and flow, just like our human ones do.

Of course, we know that God never moves away from us. We just may not sense His presence as strongly some days. And on those days, we have two choices: we can give up, or we can shake things up! We can try a different way of connecting and see what happens. We can seek out a new experience and look for Him in it, trusting that He knows our hearts and delights in our efforts to draw close to Him.

Reflect

Where's your favorite place to pray, and why?

What's your biggest struggle when it comes to setting aside time to connect with God?

Has your experience of prayer changed over time? If so, how?

In what ways have your physical senses helped to give you more meaningful prayer experiences?

What's one creative way you might connect with God today?

Respond

Next time you're having trouble entering into prayer, think about trying something new. What about a change in your environment? How can your senses help you to experience God's presence in a different way? Try playing a song that moves you—whether it makes you get up and dance or brings tears to your eyes and tugs at your heart every time you hear it. Maybe nature is your thing—get outside and feel the grass under your feet, see an endless sky full of billowy clouds or shining stars above you, and let it become a moment of praise. Soak in the warmth of a tub, write a poem, or watch children playing in a park (go down the slide if it brings your heart joy). Make yourself the coldest glass of lemonade on a hot day and savor the sweetness.

God gave us these bodies so that we might experience Him in countless ways on this earth. And while we may *think* we know what's going to happen in those set-aside times of prayer, sometimes our commitment to meet with Him takes us in new directions. Sometimes He leads us into experiences that are beyond words so we can simply be present with Him—and He, with us. Those can be times when we feel His love deeply, in ways we never expected. They are moments of true connection that grow from the fertile soil of surrender—just showing up with our whole selves and trusting Him to do the rest. And the more we practice simply showing up, the more natural it will become. Even our everyday lives with Him can be a beautiful adventure.

Self-compassion is simply giving the same kindness to ourselves that we would give to others.

CHRISTOPHER GERMER

Loving You

One way that we experience God's compassion for us is *through* us. It can take a minute for that thought to sink in, and it's difficult to comprehend sometimes! While our heavenly Father calls us to share His love with everyone we meet, we must never forget that we, ourselves, are on that list! Our relationship with ourselves is more important than we may realize. In fact, it's been said that it sets the tone for every other relationship in our lives. What do you think? How much do you enjoy your own company? How often do you remind yourself of those wonderful, God-given qualities you possess? And how often do you find reasons to criticize or devalue yourself? If you're like many people, you know how it feels to be your own best friend *and* your own worst enemy at times.

Often people who are hard on themselves are also critical of others (either vocally or silently). Of course that's not true of everyone, but when we are heavy on self judgement, it will usually affect our relationships in one way or another. Our inner world will often be reflected in our outer world, and if we seek to build healthy connections with others, we need to begin within.

The Bible reminds us that what is hidden within us will always be revealed in our actions somehow. That's just how we were created! Think about Jesus. We talk a lot about His outreach to others, but it's easy to forget how important those alone times must've been for Him. He had to develop a strong sense of Himself and His purpose. Instead of being hindered by the inner turmoil of self-criticism and doubt, He learned to value Himself as God's Son and to take care of His own needs, which allowed Him to connect with others freely and love without conditions. Jesus loved Himself in a healthy way, and we can too.

Reflect

What is your daily inner dialogue like? Would you say you often look for the best or the worst in yourself? Why do you think that is?

_____

_____

How often do you remember to pat yourself on the back? When was the last time you did so?

_____

_____

Are there times when you seem to be highly critical of others? Do you think your critical mindset might reflect how you feel about yourself? Explain.

_____

_____

How do you think Jesus' acceptance of Himself showed up in His relationships?

_____

_____

What's one step that you can take to nurture your relationship with yourself?

_____

_____

Respond

No matter how you feel about yourself today, one thing is undeniably true: you are a unique and beloved creation of God who belongs here on this earth, at this time in history. And that's no small thing! If you feel like you've honored that truth in your life, how wonderful! Keep doing what you're doing. But if you think maybe that person looking back at you in the mirror could use a little more care, then why not take a few small steps in that direction?

Take a few minutes to prayerfully consider how you feel on a typical day. Do you feel at home in yourself with a sense of peace, or is there a critic lurking, always pointing out your flaws and missteps? Do you enjoy spending time alone, or do you feel like you're sitting with a stranger sometimes?

Think about the needs you have that aren't being met right now. Are there a few of them that you could start meeting for yourself? Maybe you need more rest, or better boundaries, or a regular grocery store run for healthy stuff so you can stop berating yourself for sneaking junk food! Often, that inner critical voice just needs a little attention. The more we befriend ourselves and learn to listen more intentionally, the less that voice feels the need to shout.

When we sense the need to feel God's loving care, let us never forget the ways He may be calling us to show it to ourselves. There's great comfort and healing to be found in our own hearts as we draw near to Him and allow Him to love us *through* us. That's a gift we can give ourselves at any moment in our lives.

How we spend our days is, of course, how we spend our lives.

ANNIE DILLARD

This Is the Day

Sometimes we miss what God is providing for us in the moment because we're looking right past it. We don't mean to, of course, but we can often be distracted by an ideal future that many of us create in our minds called "someday." Sound familiar? If "someday" was an actual day, it would be jam-packed for a lot of us. We'd be finishing our to-do lists, achieving our most cherished dreams, and doing those things that for years we've been promising ourselves we would do. We'd finally get to stop, look back, and say, "Wow, that was a busy life. I'm sure glad *someday* is here so I can take a breather!" Oh, how much potential that day would hold, if only it were real. Many of us wait for it like a train that never comes.

But there's another day that's infinitely more promising than that one. It's a day that shows up quite often—a day that holds exactly what God knows we need. It is filled with many opportunities and reasons to be grateful. And if we need to get something done, it offers twenty-four hours to choose from. That day is called *today*.

The Bible reminds us of the significance of today in this oft-quoted, well-loved verse: "This is the day that the Lord has made; let us rejoice and be glad in it" (Psalm 118:24 ESV). At some point in adulthood it may truly hit us how fleeting our time on earth is compared to the eternity that stretches beyond it. And while the gift of heaven is priceless beyond words, there are many specific reasons, large and small, that we are here now. By the time you turn eighty, you will have lived nearly thirty thousand days, and you can be sure that every morning you wake up to live another one of them, your Maker has plans for you. Plans to bless you, lead you, help you grow, and remind you just how near He is—not *someday*, but *this* day.

Reflect

What's one thing you've always said you'd do "someday," and why do you think it hasn't happened?

_____

_____

Do you feel like you're more of a carpe diem person or a procrastinator—
or maybe somewhere in between? Explain.

_____

_____

What is something that's happened in your life that reminded you
of how precious your time on earth really is?

_____

_____

Do you feel like you have a sense of purpose in your days, or do you find yourself wishing
you had more clarity about your life's direction?

_____

_____

How can you sense God's presence with you in this moment?

_____

_____

Respond

One way to find more peace and contentment in our days is to pause once in a while and look at how we're spending them. Of course, no two days will ever be alike. Even if we have a fairly set schedule, life will always bring the unexpected. But if we step back and really look at our daily habits, the motions we go through, and how we tend to connect with others, we might find some things we want to adjust. Maybe the dream we've been putting off until "someday" could be realized bit by bit if we just pencil in some regular time to devote to it. Maybe we'll discover that some of the time we spend on our screens could be better spent nurturing non-virtual, face-to-face, soul-filling connections. Instead of offering people "should-vitations" (Hey, we should get together soon!), we could follow through and make it happen.

Consider spending some time in prayer, reflecting on what makes up your daily life. Maybe write it out a little so you can get a good glimpse of the things that tend to fill those precious, twenty-four-hour gifts of time you're given. Lay out that calendar of yours and offer it to God with a simple prayer like "Lord, here is the time You've given me. Am I using it wisely? Help me to make the changes necessary to live each day more fully."

As author Gretchen Rubin reminds us, "The days are long, but the years are short." And the older we get, the more we understand the truth of that. We all look back sometimes and think, "Where did the time go?" Let's ask God to help us make the most of our days so that as we reflect on our lives, we can know that we did all we could with the time we were given.

We don't see things
as they are,
we see them as we are.

ANAÏS NIN

The Beauty of Perspective

The way we're experiencing our lives today has a lot to do with how we're looking at them. And if we find ourselves praying for a lighter heart and calmer spirit, it helps to consider the role we play in receiving what God has to offer. Here's an illustration for you: When you were little, did you ever lie on the grass, look up at passing clouds in the sky, and make up stories about them? (Or maybe you still do!) Some cloudy days are perfect for that. We all see something different in the clouds, depending on our unique perspectives.

Life is similar to cloud gazing when you think about it. Everything we see and experience will be interpreted by each of us in our own way. Whether an object, an event, or a person's behavior—whatever it is that we witness outside of us is seen through a filter that exists within us.

We're always bringing a story to the table—even if we don't realize it—and that story is made up of our beliefs, our past experiences, and even whatever mood we happen to be in at a given moment.

The Bible reminds us to pay attention to *how* we're seeing, not just what we're seeing. If we're quick to judge someone, where is that coming from? Are we looking through the lens of our own opinions and expectations? Or how about when we face a challenge in our lives and we're feeling discouraged? How are we looking at that challenge? Are we automatically expecting the worst, or are we leaving room for possibility? Can we make it a regular practice to look for all the ways God can work in these situations—opening us up to possibility, teaching us something new, and even blessing us unexpectedly? Those passing "clouds" in our lives can take many forms, and we always have the freedom to choose how we will see them.

Reflect

*Are you aware of how much your imagination can play into your daily life—
both positively and negatively? How have you noticed this?*

_____

_____

*Recall an experience that involved a misperception or miscommunication.
What did you imagine was going on versus what was actually happening?*

_____

_____

*When have you jumped to a false conclusion in a situation, and how did that play out?
Next time you catch yourself creating a negative story about a situation,
how can you remind yourself to give it more time to unfold?*

_____

_____

*Who is one of the most openhearted, open-minded people in your life,
and what have they taught you?*

_____

_____

Respond

Becoming more aware of the filter we're looking through can help us respond thoughtfully rather than react carelessly to the people and situations in our lives. Try to make it a regular practice in the coming days to notice how your thoughts give meaning to your experiences. Especially when you face a relationship challenge or an unexpected situation, you may discover some familiar patterns in how you interpret things.

Of course you don't have to try and turn every "lemony" situation into lemonade. Some things are just downright tough to deal with, and some days, we all need the space to feel upset or discouraged for a bit—maybe vent some frustration or have a good cry. We're not ready for that look-on-the-bright-side speech quite yet, and that's perfectly okay. We can give ourselves grace for those cloudy thoughts, knowing that God loves us on our grouchy days just as much as on our bright, cheerful days.

But one thing we can *always* do, no matter how we feel, is leave room for God to show up. We can take a moment and prayerfully acknowledge both the reality of the situation and the hope we always have in Him: "Lord, this is hard, and I feel discouraged. But I know You are always at work." That's it. We don't have to pump ourselves up or pretend to be "over it"; we can simply acknowledge that God always plays a big part in whatever story is unfolding. As long as we keep our eyes on Him, we can trust that everything else will be resolved in due time.

In a world
where you can
be anything,
be yourself.

ETTA TURNER

The Gift of Being You

One way we can experience God's peace more fully in our lives is by living more authentically—being true to who He created us to be. There's an old tale that illustrates this truth beautifully. It's about a mouse who lives in a little cottage in the forest. The mouse spends her days knitting sweaters, chopping firewood, and gathering nuts and berries to store for the winter. She has an instinct to do these things, and she finds great purpose in them. Some of the other forest creatures tease her about being an oddball; they wonder why she doesn't get out more and frolic like they do. But she pays them no mind. Soon, winter comes with blizzards and below-zero temperatures. It's the worst in years, and the animals are unprepared and freezing. They remember the mouse and imagine the warm clothes, blazing fires, and pantry full of food she must have after all that preparation. They knock on her door, and she welcomes them with kindness and provides all they need to survive the winter.

Why is this story important? God created each of us with a particular mix of abilities, desires, and natural tendencies—just like the mouse in the story. We each have things we've always been drawn to and felt the pull to pursue. These unique traits may have been discovered and nurtured when we were children, or they may have been misunderstood and dismissed. Some of them were likely more socially acceptable than others, so we may have allowed some traits to shine, while sweeping the others under the rug. But no matter how much we have allowed ourselves to live out who we are, those God-given treasures we carry within us will never go away. He waits patiently for us to discover them and share them with the world. You can never fully comprehend the gift you're giving those around you by simply being yourself.

Reflect

What are the earliest dreams and desires you remember having as a child?

_____

_____

Were you encouraged to follow your own path, or did you feel heavily influenced by others' ideas of what your life should look like?

_____

_____

Have there been things in your life you've felt compelled to do or make but you haven't done because they seemed strange or impractical? If so, explain below.

_____

_____

Describe a time when you were just being yourself, doing your thing, and it made a surprising impact on someone else.

_____

_____

Have you ever found yourself looking at another person's life and judging it as odd, not realizing that they may simply be doing what they were made for?

_____

_____

Because we can't see the big picture, it can be tough at times to understand why we feel a nudge toward certain things in life. Maybe there's a career path that we thought was too late to take, but the desire has never left our hearts. Maybe it's a hobby we've always felt naturally drawn to or a skill we want to develop. We might have a gift for connecting with certain populations of people and we feel compelled to reach out to them. Regardless of whether others understand what we're up to, we can trust that we're feeling those things for a reason, and we can always take them to God in prayer.

How about you? How aware are you of your gifts, passions, and dreams? Pay close attention to what lights you up and brings joy to your life and to those abilities that seem to come naturally to you. Is there anything you feel particularly drawn to but aren't sure how to pursue? Take some time in prayer to ask for help discerning the things God may be calling you to. If you ask, you can always trust that He'll make those things clear in His time.

Of course, the more you're operating out of the gifts He has given you and pursuing the dreams He has placed in your heart, the more satisfying your life will be. And the more purpose you'll find—just like the little mouse—as doors open that only your Maker could see ahead of time. And here's something else we can all do: support others on their journeys, no matter how unusual their lives seem to us. We can remember how vastly different God's plan can look in every life and encourage one another to go in whatever way He leads.

When you rest,
you catch your breath,
and it fills your lungs
and holds you up,
like water wings.

ANNE LAMOTT

A Time to Rest

"And on the seventh day God ended His work which He had done, and He rested" (Genesis 2:2 NKJV). We sometimes hear this Bible verse referenced when people talk about feeling depleted. It's hard to deny the importance of setting aside time in our lives to reflect and recharge. It takes humility to admit that we can't do everything all the time! We were created with a need to pause, and as many of us have experienced, our physical and mental health will suffer if we ignore that need for too long.

So, how are you finding comfort in rest these days? Are you getting what you need? And what does "rest" look like to you? We each have our own answer to that question, and it's always changing, depending on what season of life we are in. That's why it's so important for us to tune in regularly to ourselves and listen to what our minds and bodies are truly calling for when it comes to downshifting.

It may be as simple as committing to eight hours of sleep for a while (which can be a challenge for those of us who often burn the candle at both ends). It could be giving ourselves a screen limit to reduce the amount of noise that's coming in every day and maybe reaching for a book instead—one we know will feed our spirit. It may be setting aside some time to sit outdoors in our favorite beautiful spot or designating a family day that's all about relaxing together without an agenda. It may be many different things over the years, depending on circumstances and life stages, but one thing it can *always* be is a priority in our lives. Rest is one of those gifts we give ourselves that will benefit us for a lifetime.

Reflect

How did rest and relaxation happen in the family you grew up in?
Was it considered laziness, or did your caretakers recognize the need for balance?

_____

_____

What are some telltale signs that you are getting low on rest—
whether that be a lack of sleep at night or a lack of daily down time?

_____

_____

Who in your life seems to prioritize self-care, and is there anything you've learned from them
that you might incorporate into your own rhythm?

_____

_____

What are some messages—positive or negative—that our culture gives us about rest?

_____

_____

What are some things that the Bible teaches about the importance of rest?

_____

_____

Respond

Find a peaceful place to sit with a journal or notebook and maybe even your calendar. Think about the balance you experience in your daily life. Are you on the go most of the time? Do you feel like you have room to breathe—a margin of downtime that allows you to recharge when you need to? If not, do you think you could find a few places on your calendar to pencil in a small, regular window of intentional rest? Maybe it's setting aside a half hour of quiet time just a few days a week and making the promise to stick to it—like a date you keep with yourself. Or a few nights when you could commit to getting just one extra hour of sleep.

Even the smallest steps can add up to a big change in your sense of well-being. Plus, making a commitment to yourself and keeping it reminds you that you are so worth taking care of—and your Creator backs that up 100 percent! "And the very hairs on your head are all numbered. . . . You are more valuable to God than a whole flock of sparrows" (Luke 12:7 NLT). Finding rest may involve asking for a little help from a spouse, friend, or family member. But always remember that you'd happily do the same to support them in caring for themselves (and you probably have).

Wherever you are right now, reading this, take a moment to breathe in and out as slowly and deeply as you can. Do you feel how your body is filled with a sense of calm as you come back to yourself in this moment? That's how our whole lives can feel, more and more, as we learn to live with the life-giving rhythm of rest.

*Faith means believing
in advance what will only
make sense in reverse.*

PHILIP YANCEY

Unexpected Outcomes

L et this truth find its way to your heart, and remind yourself of it often: You can trust God with every detail of your life, even when you don't quite understand what He's up to. Things may not (and probably won't) unfold exactly as you expect, but He will *never* let you down.

Have you ever hoped and prayed for something so much and had a strong feeling it was going to work out? Maybe you asked for guidance and saw signs that seemed to point you down a particular path. Or you heard a great message that lined up perfectly with your plan. You felt hopeful and certain, but then, for whatever reason, things went in a different direction. Maybe you wondered: *How did I miss it? What did I do wrong?* And most significantly: *What happens next time? Will I be afraid to step out in faith again?*

Times like these can leave us feeling discouraged and disappointed. But they can also do something unexpectedly wonderful for us: they can draw us closer to God if we are willing to bring our hurting hearts to Him. We can be completely honest with Him about how we're feeling—disappointed, confused, frustrated. And in that honesty, our connection with Him is strengthened. That's how relationships work, right? The more we communicate, the closer we become. And sometimes, it's the tough things in life that help to create the deepest connections between us.

Reflect

Describe an experience that caused you to struggle with doubt or disappointment.
Were you eventually able to see purpose in it?

_____

_____

Do you ever feel overly cautious when it comes to stepping out in faith based on past experiences?

_____

_____

Is there anything you're trusting God for right now? Do you need a gentle reminder
that He knows exactly what's best for you, regardless of the outcome? Ask Him for it here.

_____

_____

Do you have a few people in your life whom you can trust to help you prayerfully discern your path?
List them here.

_____

_____

Who in your life today could use a little encouragement about stepping out in faith
and trusting God to handle the results?

_____

_____

Respond

Here's one thing you may have heard about prayers: *they're always answered, just not always how we expect.* Next time you're feeling disheartened about an unanswered prayer, instead of allowing a cloud of discouragement to settle in, why not use it as an opportunity to really dig in and draw close to God? He wants nothing more than for us to seek His heart in every circumstance. Ask everything you can think to ask! *Why did it happen this way? What am I supposed to see in this? How can it teach me more about myself and about You?*

There are things He is waiting to show us, discoveries He's inviting us to make, and burdens He wants to free us from. And sometimes, life plays out the way it does for those very reasons. Nothing is wasted in God's economy. It's okay that we cling sometimes to certain outcomes—we're human! But never forget that there's something infinitely greater happening on the journey of prayer. We are being given opportunities to become more and more like Christ, and sometimes that looks different than what we might imagine it to be!

Next time you have a need to step out in faith—even if uncertainty creeps up—remind yourself that it's safe to step out boldly anyway with confidence that God knows exactly what's up. Just go in the direction you're led, and know that no matter how hard you knock, He will only open doors that are best for you to walk through, and He'll close the ones that aren't.

Most importantly, in the process, you'll learn more about Him and about who He's created you to be. And that's what this faith journey is all about.

*It is amazing
what you can accomplish
if you do not care
who gets the credit.*

HARRY S. TRUMAN

Serving God Alone

Sometimes God invites us to look within ourselves for what we've been depending on others to provide. This is especially true when it comes to being recognized or appreciated for something we've done. Whether we've achieved a small act of service or a significant accomplishment, receiving a pat on the back or an expression of gratitude can be wonderful—an encouraging reminder that our efforts haven't gone unnoticed. But there are times in our lives (parenthood, volunteering, or even our jobs outside our homes) when we work hard to provide something, and there's no fanfare involved. Maybe not even a "Thank you!" or "Great job!" to be heard. As discouraging as these times can be, they can also be blessings in disguise. How? They point us toward the One who *does* see and appreciate every little effort we make in our lives—every sacrifice, every late night, every early morning we give, and every goal we painstakingly achieve.

Our heavenly Father delights in the good things we do, just as we delight in seeing the children in our lives learn to serve others and accomplish new things. But we know that if those children grow up forever looking for someone else to validate their efforts, they'll live with a lot of disappointment. They need to learn to appreciate themselves, even when no one else is watching. And there's a gift we can give them that God provides for all of us—the ability to celebrate our own growth and to recognize our own accomplishments, regardless of who else notices. We can experience joy in the fact that the One who matters most sees it all.

Reflect

Are you someone who doesn't mind working behind the scenes with little recognition, or do you find yourself wishing for more appreciation for your efforts? Explain.

_____

_____

Do you remember what it felt like growing up, hoping for someone to notice or appreciate you? How has this pattern persisted in your adult life?

_____

_____

Can you think of the last time you put a lot of effort toward something that no one seemed to notice? How did you deal with it?

_____

_____

Are there a few verses you might find or recall to serve as reminders that God sees and cares deeply about the details of your life? Write them here.

_____

_____

Is there anyone you know who seems genuinely satisfied with doing things without recognition? What do you notice about their life?

_____

_____

Respond

Here's something to try in the coming days: do a few things on purpose that you know you won't be recognized for. It could be as simple as taking a loop on the walking trail in your neighborhood to pick up trash or paying for the person behind you in the drive-through. It could be setting a personal goal for yourself that you've been wanting to accomplish and then celebrating it quietly in your heart when you achieve it. Maybe have a little one-person "woo-hoo" moment! Turn some music up loud and dance for the joy of it, or treat yourself to that over-the-top, decadent coffee drink and savor every sip. Feel the sense of confidence you're building within, and soak in the satisfaction of a job well done.

Letting our personal experience of something be enough, without having to post about it on social media or have others notice it, is a good practice for all of us. It helps to strengthen our humility muscle, which can bring us a lot of peace—because we waste less and less energy trying to be noticed and validated. It reminds us whose loving attention really matters in the end. Our heavenly Father cares deeply about our growth and surely takes great joy in our accomplishments. He will always be our audience of One. So next time you do something worthy of a pat on the back and find yourself waiting for one, reach right back there and do it yourself. Thank Him for being present in every detail of your life, and enjoy that moment of recognition within.

Transformation is a process . . . a journey of discovery.

RICK WARREN

Your Own Pace

I would bet that you've heard a butterfly metaphor or two in your time—and for good reason! Many of us needing hope and reassurance in our lives have been inspired by the miraculous metamorphosis that takes place in nature—from caterpillar to cocoon and beyond. You may also have heard about how the body of that caterpillar breaks down to almost nothing before being reorganized into the winged wonder that emerges. God's creation is amazing!

And while the same kind of thing happens for us on the faith journey, we can sometimes forget how gradual it can be. The incredible change that occurs for that cocooned creature in a few weeks is actually the journey of a lifetime for us. When we make the decision to follow Jesus, there's usually not a sudden moment when we can exclaim, "Ta-da! Check out the brand-new me!" Transformation occurs one day at a time, for the rest of our lives. But unlike the caterpillar, we don't have to wait for some big emergence or moment of arrival to see evidence of our beautiful transformation. We have the gift of witnessing the ways God is showing up in our lives every day—helping us grow, shedding light on the things we need to let go of for our freedom, and turning our raw material, bit by bit, into something we never imagined possible.

It's so important that we remember this process takes time, especially when we find ourselves discouraged about falling back into some of the same old patterns that we thought we'd moved past for good. Whatever He's allowing us to face again could be for our further healing. If something keeps coming up, that could be God's way of saying, "It's okay—just pay attention. We're still transforming this."

Reflect

What's the most significant step of faith you feel you've ever taken,
and how have you seen your life change since then?

_____

_____

What things within yourself do you feel most discouraged about—
maybe struggles you hoped would be "over" by now?

_____

_____

What changes have you seen in yourself most recently (even small ones) that you are grateful for?

_____

_____

What's one way you feel God may be calling you to take a step toward change in your life today?

_____

_____

Is there anyone you know who is struggling with something personal right now?
How can you encourage them?

_____

_____

Sometimes on these transformation journeys of ours, we run into the "shoulds." Have you ever heard of them? They're demeaning, persistent thoughts that like to remind us of all we haven't yet become. They tell us who we *should* be and what we *should* be doing and how we *should* have parts of our lives put together by now! Sometimes the "shoulds" become so familiar we forget that they're even in our subconscious, constantly casting a shadow and causing us to doubt that true change is actually happening in our lives. But the reality is that true change is *always* happening within us. Since the day we trusted Christ, it's been happening—even in those times when we can't see it ourselves. And when we observe the lives of others, let's remember the same thing: only God can see what's going on in that cocoon of theirs, regardless of what their actions look like to us.

One powerful thing that we can do to help ourselves stay strong is to fill our hearts with the encouragement found in God's Word. Then when the "shoulds" do come calling, and we feel that familiar pull toward discouragement, we can resist it. We can have a kind of arsenal of eternal truth to help protect us from temporary doubt. Consider gathering promises from the Bible that focus on your transformation in Christ. In II Corinthians 4:16, Paul reminds us to "not lose heart" because "inwardly we are being renewed day by day" (NIV). You could create an affirming reminder or two to speak with confidence during times of self-doubt: "My life is unfolding beautifully in God's time, in God's way." Remember, it's not about being where we *should* be; it's about being where He has brought us today. And tomorrow, we can trust that He'll lead us a little further on.

Burnout is what happens when you try to avoid being human for too long.

MICHAEL GUNGOR

Taking Care of You

Self-care chatter is everywhere these days, and maybe that's because we need it more than ever in a world that seems to move at lightning speed. Caring for our minds and bodies requires intention, and when we find ourselves feeling overwhelmed or discouraged in some way, it's good to consider how well we've been caring for ourselves and how much it can affect our overall sense of well-being.

Burnout is a real thing, after all, and most of us have experienced it to some degree in our lives. Sometimes it creeps up and hits us out of nowhere; other times, it shows up slowly and gradually. It may be the result of a demanding career, a strenuous season of parenthood, saying yes to too many opportunities, or just being hit with a lot of things at once. Many of us feel it to the extreme. We reach a breaking point, drop into a chair somewhere, and think, *I just can't do this anymore.*

Those can be some of life's toughest moments because of how completely tapped out and powerless we feel. But they can *also* be the most hopeful points of our journeys because they remind us of the wonderful truth that there really *is* a God—and He is *definitely* not us! It is often at the end of our rope that we experience His presence most profoundly.

If you find yourself feeling this kind of soul-deep weariness (or even feeling momentarily overwhelmed), always remember that it will pass, even if you can't imagine it right now. We're sometimes allowed to reach those breaking points so we can truly grasp the importance of caring for these bodies, minds, and hearts God that has given us. And so we can remember that our true sustenance will always be found in Him.

Reflect

When have you come to a place of burnout in your life—a time when you felt completely exhausted and discouraged? How do you think it happened?

What are some ways you feel overextended right now, and is there anything (even a small thing) you can do to help yourself find more balance?

Do you know anyone who seems frazzled or overwhelmed currently, and if so, is there a way you can support them?

What are some Bible verses that speak to finding rest in God? Write them here.

What are some ways you can proactively protect yourself from reaching a breaking point?

Respond

There are small things we can do for ourselves every day to help maintain balance in our lives and avoid heading down the path toward burnout. We can start by making sure we're incorporating plenty of self-care—whether that be scheduling naps, taking walks, or promising ourselves a relaxing bath at the end of the day. We can make it a regular practice to pause before saying yes to a new opportunity. Often, a simple "Can I let you know tomorrow?" or "I need to pray about that" is all we need to ensure that we're listening to our gut and God's guidance.

When we *do* start to feel overwhelmed, instead of ignoring it and just hoping it'll pass, we can take the time to pay attention to where it might be coming from. It could simply be that we have too much on our plates! If this happens to you, consider looking at all you're trying to accomplish at once, and see where you might let a few things go—or at least cut them in half. Does *all* the laundry need to be done right now? Can you ask someone else to pick up the kids today? Can you just be honest and say, "I need to reschedule this coffee date because I'm exhausted, and I'd rather connect with you when I can be my best self"? If you have a hard time hurting someone's feelings by saying no, remember—you've heard that word before and survived. The people in your life will too! And if you hate to burden others by asking for help, just recall how good you felt the last time you were able to bless someone by showing up for *them*. We're all in this together, and your well-being is just as important as the well-being of every other person on the planet. May you never forget that.

There are two ways of spreading light: to be the candle or the mirror that reflects it.

EDITH WHARTON

Let Them Shine

Some of us have had the lyrics to the song "This Little Light of Mine" memorized since our earliest childhood years. Others learned later in life that Jesus is the Light of the World and that we are all called to reflect His light. Regardless, we got the gist of it at some point—we're called to open our hearts and allow Him to shine through us in ways that we could never muster on our own. Of course, this involves finding opportunities to share His love and using the gifts God has given us to bless the people around us.

But it also means helping *others* find ways to shine. And in the world today, we may know a few people in our communities whose light has dimmed a bit. It's possible they've been in survival mode in some way, and we may know from experience that when that happens, we humans often don't have much energy to look outward. In fact, they may seem downright self-centered. But the truth is, they're just trying to do whatever they can to hold it together.

There are also folks in our lives right now who just haven't found a way to let the light come through. They may feel the desire to reach out, connect, and make a difference in some way, but they have no idea where to start. Helping people to share their light can be one of the most rewarding experiences on our faith journey. It's a little taste of God's kingdom—living as we're meant to live, helping one another find the fullest expressions of our lives in Him.

Reflect

Who would you say has been most influential in helping you to shine your light in the world?

_____

_____

Do you remember a time of feeling hesitant or unsure about how you might share God's love with those around you? What was it like?

_____

_____

Have you noticed how in challenging times some people feel inspired to reach out more and others tend to withdraw? Can you think of a recent example?

_____

_____

Who in your life seems to have a "dim" light right now, and do you have any idea what they might be dealing with behind the scenes?

_____

_____

What's one simple thing you could do to encourage that person to reach out and use their gifts for good?

_____

_____

Respond

Sometimes we shine the brightest for God when we help someone else to uncover their light. It's not about trying to fix them or point out their missed opportunities. It *is* about encouraging them, reminding them of their unique gifts, and inviting them to open their hearts to new possibilities. If you feel drawn to encourage someone, ask God for the best timing. Ask Him to give you the words they most need to hear to inspire them—not just the words you think they need. Ask for courage to speak the truth in love.

If this isn't something you've even thought about before, you're not alone! Many of us are so busy just figuring out how to walk our *own* path that we haven't noticed that someone beside us may have hidden their lamp under a basket (Matthew 5:15). So take a look around at the light you see coming from others. Do you notice potential in someone who may just need a little nudge or vote of confidence?

Children, especially, are often unaware of the difference they can make in the world—even through simple gestures of kindness at home or in school. When there seems to be a lot of fear or uncertainty in the atmosphere, their pure prayers, colorful creations, and bright smiles can bless people so beautifully. Sometimes kids (and grown-ups too) just need to be reminded of the gifts God has given them to bless the world in their unique ways. Let's make it a point to lift someone up today and help them along the path to discovering all they're created to be.

The grass is greener

where you water it.

NEIL BARRINGHAM

Grateful for What Is

Gratitude is like a balm for our spirits. It can bring us deep satisfaction in our lives, regardless of our circumstances. It transfers our focus from what we *don't* have to what we *do* have. Gratitude is a little shift that our hearts can make anytime toward God's goodness—a little shift that can make a big difference. And that's extra important for us to remember when we're dealing with a struggle that no one likes to face: *envy*. Envy is something we all encounter at times in life. We may try to hide it. Ignore it. Beat ourselves up for feeling it. And even wonder, *Good grief. Why can't I see that the grass is just as green over here?*

The grass will always be greenest where we water it! How do we water our grass and appreciate God's blessings in our lives? With our praise. We take a good look at what we do have in our lives, and we find ways to say, "Thank You." *Thank You, Lord, for this blessing. This job. This opportunity. This home that may be small or messy, but it's still my haven. This body that may be imperfect, but it's the one You gave me and I'm doing the best I can to care for it.* The more we take our eyes off what others possess (which can be tough these days when it's coming at us from everywhere), the more we can find contentment, right where we are, with what we have.

And please hear this: Contentment doesn't mean settling for less, giving up on our dreams, or never striving for more in life. It just means that *first* we find a firm foundation in what God has provided for us today and in who He has uniquely created us to be. *Then* we can look over our fence with appreciation for everyone and everything else without growing envious!

Reflect

When was the last time you recall feeling envious of someone?

_____

_____

Have you ever felt frustrated or maybe even resentful about not having a particular thing?
If so, what was it and did you ever get it?

_____

_____

Describe a time when online media, TV, or magazines contributed to a "grass is greener" feeling for you.

_____

_____

What are some reasons to be grateful in your life right now, just as it is?

_____

_____

What are a few Bible verses that speak to the importance of letting go of envy? Write them here.

_____

_____

Respond

One thing that *doesn't* help when we find ourselves feeling discontented, ungrateful, or just downright frustrated about what's missing in our lives is to beat ourselves up for feeling that way. Remember that it's something that happens to all of us! But the good news is that once we become aware that we're headed down the path of jealousy, we can start taking steps in a more positive direction. Here are a few ideas:

Be creative: Sit down with your journal, reflect on your life, and challenge yourself to make a list of blessings you've never considered before. Then, take a moment to thank God for those things.

Shift your focus: If you're aware of the people and things (especially online) that bring up a sense of envy in your life, try reducing your exposure to them. Maybe step away for a set amount of time, redirect your energy elsewhere, and see what happens for you.

Flip the script: Try a completely different approach if it feels right to you! If there is a certain someone in your life who seems to trigger you in this area, try moving *toward* them instead of away. Find ways to genuinely appreciate this person as a unique creation of God. Maybe even commit to praying for this person in the coming days. Chances are, once you shift gears, you'll recognize that they are just as human as you are and have just as many struggles as strengths.

And most importantly, you can offer a simple prayer anytime, like this one: *Lord, thank You for my life, just as it is. Help me to deeply appreciate all You have provided. Wake me up to the blessings that go unnoticed every day. I want to live a life full of contentment and gratitude. Amen.*

Listening is about being present, not just about being quiet.

KRISTA TIPPETT

Is Anyone Listening?

These days, when words seem plentiful, silence can be precious and rare. As our phones light up with messages and the internet buzzes with new content, finding some quiet for our minds and hearts can feel like a true respite—especially when we're dealing with tough things in our lives. In fact, sometimes what we really need is someone to sit with us in that silence and hear our hearts. What a gift the presence of a true listener can be. Not someone who's waiting for their turn to talk, or coming up with ideas to fix us, or even thinking up some verses to inspire us. Of *course*, it's wonderful to be on the receiving end of encouragement. But some moments simply call for a loving witness to be with us in our times of struggle.

James 1:19 reminds us to be "quick to listen" and "slow to speak." The people in our lives who are able to do both are true blessings. If we don't have any supportive listeners in our lives, it's never too late to ask God to bring someone along. And we, in turn, can be that kind of support for others. When someone comes to us with a problem and needs to vent or just tell their story, we can practice the patience of truly listening. If we're in the habit of searching for solutions or trying to help fix things as quickly as possible, we can try something different. We can take a breath, take in everything they're saying, and allow them the space to feel it all before we respond. Those moments of silence may clear the way for God to speak to both of our hearts.

Reflect

Who is the best listener in your life, and what is an example of how they've blessed you with their presence?

When someone seeks you out for support, how do you tend to respond— with more listening, or more advice, or both? Explain.

What's one small adjustment you would like to make to the quality of your conversations?

Can you find a few examples of how the Bible speaks to the importance of listening? Write them here.

Who is someone in your life right now who might need a listening ear? Would you consider setting aside a little time to reach out to them?

Respond

You can learn a lot about yourself by paying close attention to your conversations with others. Do you feel like there's a good balance in your exchanges, or do you often get the sense that you're not really being heard? Do you wish you had more intentional listeners in your life? Sometimes it's simply about finding the courage to ask for what you need in your current relationships. Even your closest loved ones may not be aware of how you're feeling, and they would surely want to know the best way they can support you—especially in tough times.

If you don't feel you have good listeners in your inner circle, ask God to help you share that need with those who love you. You might also consider investing in more connections with people who can provide some patient, quiet encouragement when you need it. As most of us have experienced, a few intentional words spoken at the right time can be much more effective than an outpouring of well-meaning but careless words of advice.

And on the flip side, think about how you show up for others. Pay attention to your conversations in the days to come and see what your natural tendencies are. Do you form an answer before others finish talking? Are you comfortable allowing a pause, or do you feel the need to fill it up with words? And if you don't like what you observe, then take some small steps toward change. Show up differently next time. Be intentional about listening. Allow more space and see how God might work through you in the in-between.

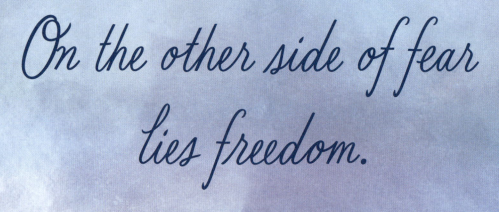

*On the other side of fear
lies freedom.*

ANONYMOUS

Freedom from Fear

We never outgrow the need for reassurance in our lives, especially when it comes to finding the courage to step out of our comfort zones. Life can bring some daunting challenges, but those challenges can be blessings in disguise. They can lead us through the forest of our fears and allow us to emerge from the other side with greater strength and confidence. It feels wonderful to look back and exclaim, "Wow, I really did it!" But as most of us have discovered, the journey from A to B isn't easy.

The words *courage* and *encouragement* share the same core idea—developing from the heart (the Latin root is *cor*). The heart is where every brave action begins. If we're open to it, that's where God will meet us in those times we feel most fearful, holding out His hand for us to take as we set out on shaky legs. Sure, we can build ourselves up—gathering all the facts, repeating affirmations, practicing incessantly, and promising ourselves great rewards for our bravery—but real courage will always start with Him working in our hearts. We can discover an indomitable spirit right at the center of who we are, inspired by these words of Jesus: "With God all things are possible" (Matthew 19:26).

Even if you're not facing something epic at this moment in your life, most days offer little opportunities to move forward in faith when you feel like retreating in fear, whether it's a conversation you've been putting off, an idea you've been reluctant to share, or just a step you've been wanting to take toward something bigger. You're always invited to visit the quiet center within, where God's reassuring presence dwells to nudge you lovingly onward.

Reflect

When was the last time you experienced something that took a lot of courage,
and what was your experience like?

_____

_____

When you're faced with something you fear, how do you tend to respond?

_____

_____

Are there any fears that seem to come up for you frequently,
and do you have any sense of where they started?

_____

_____

How do you feel when you look back at something you overcame, and how can you remind yourself
of that feeling next time you need to take a brave step in your life?

_____

_____

What are some Bible verses that speak to your heart about living courageously and letting go of fear?
Write them here.

_____

_____

Respond

Fear is so personal to each of us. The thing that takes one person every ounce of courage they can muster may be a walk in the park for another. It's easy to look at something that someone else is facing and wonder why it seems to be such a big deal to them. And on the flip side, we can be hard on ourselves sometimes, too—wondering why we can't just get over our fear and take a leap of faith. Nobody else seems to be incessantly worried about their parachute opening—what's wrong with us?

But it helps to remember that we're never comparing apples to apples. As God's unique creations, we will always have different struggles and strengths. We're just wonderfully diverse like that! And we can see the purpose in it all as we learn to live in close community with one another. Where one of us struggles, the other may be strong and able to provide the encouragement we need to see us through.

So, what can we do today? Whether or not we're facing something big at the moment, we can always build our faith muscles by reminding ourselves often of the strong foundation we stand on. We can have phrases of truth that reflect God's promises ready for moments of hesitation: *The peace of Christ is with me* (John 20:21); *God will strengthen, help, and hold me* (Isaiah 41:10); *I trust in Jesus* (John 14:1); *He delivers me from all my fears* (Psalm 34:4).

Remember: when we start to move into fear, we can feel it in our bodies. Whenever that happens for you, take a soul-deep breath and return to your calm center where the Holy Spirit waits to assure you that you have all you need within.

*Compassion opens
limitless doors
to human connection.*

STEVE GILLILAND

Building Bridges

We live in a time that can feel scary and uncertain for a lot of us because of the dissonance and division we witness around us. We're bombarded with an "us versus them" mentality. *Follow this person, not that one. Believe my story, not theirs.* It can make us feel like strangers to each other, when really, we all carry the same deep need inside—the need to feel safe, connected and loved just as we are.

About two thousand years ago, Jesus entered a world that had divided itself in many ways, between cultures, religions, and political beliefs—all things we humans still deal with today. But despite what people expected Him to do, He did quite the opposite. He didn't set out to conquer and declare the superiority of one tribe or type of person over another. He had a completely different intention, and that was to bring the love of the Father to everyone. He reached across divides, welcomed those who had been rejected, and spoke the painful truth to the ones who'd always mistakenly believed that they were better than the rest.

When we consider how we might follow Him today—bringing God's peace into the midst of division—Christ's example can be a wonderful place to start. We can step right into the crossfire of all the differing beliefs, opinions, judgments, and agendas and go straight to radically loving everyone. When we find ourselves feeling fearful or uncertain about what's happening around us, let's remember the power of what lies within us: the unconditional love of Christ for every person on the planet.

Reflect

In what ways have you witnessed a sense of division in the world around you lately?

_____

_____

Where have you seen connection and bridge building happening between people?

_____

_____

What is your favorite story from Jesus' life that illustrates His reaching out to someone, despite any barriers or the opinions of others? Write it here.

_____

_____

What's one thing you have done recently to connect with someone who needed it?

_____

_____

What's one thing you'd like to do more of?

_____

_____

Respond

There are things that each of us can do in our everyday lives to build bridges, and while many of those things may seem rather simple, they can be quite powerful—especially when we're following God's lead. He knows exactly who needs compassion and understanding the most, and how He's going to bring us together when the time is right. When we make ourselves available to carry His love into the world, there's no telling what He will do through us. And we can be sure that whatever it is, we'll be just as blessed as those on the receiving end.

Maybe we'll choose to listen to someone, even if we don't agree with their beliefs, just so they can have the chance to be heard. Maybe we'll cross cultural barriers to offer compassion to people whose lives look nothing like ours. Maybe we'll find the courage to shine a light on the ignorance and unjust actions that divide people and cause them to hurt one another. There are countless ways we can make loving connections, and the more we do so, the less fear we will live with because we will experience the powerful truth that we are all in this together.

What are some ways you might feel called to connect with others today? Spending some quiet time in God's presence, just listening to what comes to you, is a wonderful start. Also, start paying close attention to the people you cross paths with—whether online or in the real world. If you trust that God is always working behind the scenes, then you know there is no such thing as a chance meeting. Keep an open heart and listen for God's "still small voice" (I Kings 19:12 KJV) within that may prompt you to reach out to someone. Remember that you can't go wrong with a loving action, even if it seems to fall flat or isn't acknowledged or reciprocated. Our heavenly Father knows the intentions of our hearts and will always take what we offer and make something beautiful out of it. We need only to look at the life of Jesus to see what wonderful things can happen when we live as vessels of His love.

Deep breaths are like little love notes to your body.

ANONYMOUS

Inhale, Exhale

There's a reason that the age-old advice "Take a deep breath" is still around. It works! When we're trying to find peace in times of stress, a simple inhale and exhale can make a big difference. The funny thing is that we're so used to breathing, we're usually not even aware that it's happening!

If you ever want to know what's really going on in your body, try checking in with your breath. This in-and-out flow of life has accompanied you through every moment of your existence. It's like a gauge that can give you a glimpse of your inner workings at any moment. When you're stressed, your breath is probably shallow. When you're relaxed or in awe of something, it's probably long and deep. When you're afraid, it may be held in altogether! And because it's so interconnected with every part of us, our breath can be a huge help when it comes to calming ourselves in tough times.

The Bible makes many mentions of God's breath as a life force and our own breath as a gift from Him to sustain us on the earth. And we can celebrate that gift by using it to its full potential! As we spend time in prayer (which is like breathing for our spirits) we can tend to our physical selves, too, by slowing our breath and allowing it to bring stillness to our minds and bodies.

Reflect

Check in with yourself right now. Is your breathing shallow or deep?
Is it coming more from your chest or your belly? Why?

_____

_____

Describe a time you noticed your quality of breath changing today.

_____

_____

How can you remind yourself occasionally to check in with your breathing
and see how it might be reflecting what's going on within you?

_____

_____

What happens in your body when you stop and take three deep, intentional breaths?

_____

_____

Use your breath to help you find your calm center during your next quiet time in prayer.
Write about your experience.

_____

_____

Respond

Whether you took an anatomy class in school, work in healthcare, or have just observed the fascinating workings of the human body in some way, it's hard to deny that there is a Creator who orchestrated it all. And our Creator knows exactly what you need to keep your body running well. In the next 365 days, for example, you will take over eight million breaths. While most of them will happen without your awareness, you can always harness the power of those miraculous gifts to use to your advantage!

Consider this: when we encounter a stressful situation, we're often triggered to reach for certain things we've adopted over time to deal with that stress. These things have likely become habits, and for many of us, the habits can be unhealthy. Not only that—they often provide just a few minutes of relief, and then we're right back to where we started, feeling tense and overwhelmed. But deep breathing could have a much healthier, longer-lasting effect. And, in some cases, the effects can be felt immediately.

When we look to God for comfort and peace in stressful times, let's always remember that He has designed us with a wonderful way to help calm ourselves. Even slowing down for a deep inhale and exhale once in a while can contribute to a much calmer spirit over time.

And now that you don't have to be perfect, you can be good.

JOHN STEINBECK

Dear Me, Lighten Up . . .

Here's an assignment for you today: *Go easy on yourself.* Does that sound wonderful or impossible? (Or maybe a little of both?) The truth is, most of us need that reminder quite often in our lives because—drum roll, please—we're human! In fact, you don't have to get far in the Bible (once people show up on the scene) to witness a good amount of imperfection. Mistakes are made, marks are missed, and some pretty devious stuff goes down! And just like our long line of ancestors, we, too, often find ourselves falling short in our own ways—even unintentionally—even when we've tried earnestly to make changes and do better.

Once we open our eyes in the morning, it's likely that at some point during the day, we will have an imperfect moment (or several). Knowing that doesn't have to discourage us though; in fact, the more honest we are with ourselves and others about our realness, the more freedom we have to lighten up and enjoy life. It's not that we tell ourselves to ditch our standards and do whatever we want; it's just that we give ourselves permission to be human in an imperfect world while we do our best to follow Jesus. And most importantly, we remember that the God who made us sees our hearts and knows we're doing the best we can. Instead of berating us for tripping in the first place, He encourages us to dust ourselves off, get back up, and keep trying. Just do the next right thing; take one more step with Him on the journey.

If we wake up every day with a goal of perfection—in any area of our lives—we'll greatly reduce our chances of experiencing true joy, which is found by those who trust God more than they trust in their own ability to get things right. Perfectionism can paralyze us; authenticity can free us to be who we're called to be, knowing there's a safety net of grace beneath us to catch us when we fall.

Reflect

Think about what happens when you make a mistake. How hard is it for you to switch gears and move on?

_____

_____

In what ways have you struggled with perfectionism in your life?
How has it affected your ability to enjoy life?

_____

_____

Who are a few examples of people from the Bible (or maybe other faith-filled folks you know)
who struggled with great difficulty, yet God still worked through them in wonderful ways?

_____

_____

How do you react when someone else in your life makes a mistake—whether it be a child,
family member, friend, or coworker? Are you as hard on them as you are with yourself? Explain.

_____

_____

Can you think of some encouragement you might give yourself
the next time you're struggling with imperfection? Write it here.

_____

_____

Respond

One way to find grace for ourselves when we stumble is to imagine what we might say to someone we love if they were to make the same kind of misstep. It's likely we would have much more compassion for them than we do for ourselves in those moments. We might remind them of all the wonderful, positive things about themselves that they're forgetting because they're focusing so much on the negative. We might tell them that they aren't defined by their mistakes or by what anyone else perceives as being unacceptable about their lives. We might gently nudge them to pray to their loving Father, who always waits with open arms of forgiveness, comfort, and reassurance.

Here's a healing exercise: think about what you might say in a note to that person you love when they're feeling unworthy, and then take a moment and write a note like that to yourself. Maybe you haven't experienced an epic blunder in a while. Good for you! But maybe there are everyday things in your life that weigh on you, things that you feel aren't good enough or ways you struggle with perfectionism that steal your joy. Speak to yourself with tenderness and understanding, and then read what you wrote out loud and take it in. Always keep in mind that you need the same love, grace, and compassion you'd offer anyone else. You might be surprised about the transformation that can happen, little by little, as you focus less on your imperfections and more on God's goodness and grace every day.

I don't know what the future may hold, but I know who holds the future.

RALPH ABERNATHY

The Power to Choose

Close your eyes for a moment, take a deep breath, and tell yourself this beautiful truth: *All will be well.* Isn't that a wonderful reminder amid life's uncertainty? Most of us could benefit from hearing those words daily! See, we have these other two words that tend to show up in our minds every now and then: *What if?* And the thoughts that follow those words can have a significant effect on our well-being. For many of us, those thoughts tend to be fearful: *What if this doesn't go well? What if I'm not safe? What if she never returns? What if he tells everyone? What if . . . ?* Our God-given imaginations can be used for wonderful things, but when we allow them to be taken over by fear, it casts a shadow in our lives that God didn't intend to be there.

We all deal with negative expectations in our lives to some degree and for different reasons. Some of us are afraid to get our hopes up. We try imagining worst-case scenarios in order to protect ourselves from being disappointed. Others have had unexpected things happen in the past and think that by preparing themselves they won't be blindsided in the future. For whatever reason, we take the darker path in our minds sometimes. It's part of being human.

But another part of being human is our ability to choose our thoughts. We can always move those *what if* statements in a more positive direction. We just need to be intentional about it: *What if it's not as bad as I think? What if I'll be okay, no matter the outcome?* Sometimes it's simply about remembering that we have a loving Creator who gifted us with the power to choose and who is always there, desiring to help us use our imaginations for good.

Reflect

Are there some what ifs *you find yourself returning to in your mind regularly, either positive or negative? Write them here.*

_____

_____

Can you describe a time when you had to deal with uncertainty and fearful thoughts tried to take over?

_____

_____

Can you describe a time when positive thoughts helped you through a difficult time?

_____

_____

What are a few Bible verses that you might place somewhere visible or tuck into your journal (or your heart) to regularly remind you to lift your thoughts to God? Write them here.

_____

_____

Is there anyone in your life who seems to struggle with what ifs, *and is there some small way you can encourage them?*

_____

_____

Are you up for a little *what if* challenge? When those fears come to mind, start noticing the path that your thoughts naturally take. See if you can move the needle more toward expecting the best instead of the worst. We all know the outcome won't always be what we're hoping for, regardless of how much we hope for certain results. It may be disappointing or downright painful to practice hope in uncertain times. But here's what we need to remember more than anything: the most peaceful path we can ever take toward an unknown future is the one where we walk hand in hand with God. The more we learn to trust Him to lovingly provide for us today, the less we will worry about what tomorrow might bring.

Try pondering this question, maybe in prayer or on paper: What does your daily walk with God really look like? In the nitty-gritty of your day, when situations arise and fearful thoughts present themselves, how often do you stop and remind yourself that it all really *is* in His hands?

Consider making a list of all the *what ifs* that tend to weigh you down. Most of us have a few general fears that come up quite often, just in different disguises. Interview yourself about what you're truly afraid of in times of uncertainty. What are those core fears you arrive at routinely, and where did they begin? Ask for God's healing in those areas. Then, make a nice, long list of the positive *what ifs* you'd like to choose when fear comes knocking.

May it encourage you to know that there will likely be plenty of outcomes in your life that are far more wonderful than you could imagine. And when they aren't, you have a loving Father who knows exactly what you need to see you through.

Our identity rests in God's relentless tenderness for us revealed in Jesus Christ.

BRENNAN MANNING

Who Do You See?

No matter how you see yourself today, please remember this one precious thing: *You are, at your core, a child of God.* Nothing else about you will ever be more important or more beautiful about you than that truth.

You see, every day of our lives we catch glimpses of ourselves in many different mirrors, reflections that tell us who we are. Most of these mirrors aren't hanging on walls. They're a different kind of mirror altogether. They're the people in our lives who look back at us and reflect who we are in their eyes. For instance, children reflect the fact that we are much-needed caretakers; neighbors reflect the truth that our actions affect those around us because we're all connected; our bosses and coworkers reflect our responsibility to do honest work and provide for ourselves and our families.

All these connections show us different facets of who we are, and together they help to make up the way we see our place in the world. This is a wonderful dynamic that God clearly intended, as He created us to live in community with one another. Relationships help us to learn who we are and how much we matter to the people we're connected with every day.

But while these reflections can be powerful reminders of our worth, it's vital for us to remember that they do not *create* our worth and identity. Our identity is found in God alone. Our relationship with Him is the only "mirror" that reflects who we are 100 percent of the time—the clearest "mirror" of our identity and worth that we have the opportunity to look into every day. The more we see ourselves in Him, as His children, the less we depend on others to show us who we are. We can savor our relationships, honor our responsibilities, and find great purpose in our endeavors without ever depending on them alone to fulfill us and define us.

Reflect

Think of the people you interact with each day. How do they reflect part of your identity back to you?

_____

_____

If someone asked, "Who are you?" how would you respond?

_____

_____

Where do you find yourself looking for your worth apart from your identity as a child of God? Are these reliable ways of finding self-worth, or do you need to focus more on your identity as God's child?

_____

_____

How does believing your worth is based on what people think affect your life?

_____

_____

Who in your life seems strongly rooted in their relationship with God,
and what do you notice about them?

_____

_____

Respond

Whether we interact daily with many people or just a few, whether we work on the road, in an office, or in a piled-high laundry room, we're always going to see our reflection in the world around us somehow. It's just the nature of being alive here on planet Earth with the other seven billion or so souls who inhabit it at the moment!

The good news is that we get to choose how we will react to the "mirrors" that our relationships show us. The more firmly rooted we are in God's unconditional love for us, the more our identity is set. Any other facets of ourselves that we see—as workers, creators, parents, spouses, friends, neighbors, or teachers (you get the idea)—are just *parts* of who we are. Never the whole.

Pay attention to your different social roles in the next few days and notice how they help to make up the way you see yourself. Where do you tend to lean most heavily to find your identity? The Bible has much to say about the wonderful security of who we are in Christ. Consider making a "mirror list" of the many things God says about you as His child. Why not hang it up on the bathroom mirror you look into every morning? The more you focus on those unchanging aspects of yourself, the more naturally you will lean into them when you start to forget the beautiful truth of who—and whose—you really are.

Always remember,
your body is sacred.
It's the only home
God has given you
to live in all your life.

ANONYMOUS

At Home in You

This is an invitation to come home to one of the most beautiful places God has provided for you in this life—*your body*. Some of us need that invitation daily because we spend a lot of time in our heads! Consider this: How often do you realize you just did something that you have no recollection of? It could be a small task like washing a dish or starting the coffee maker. Or it might be something bigger like the phenomenon called "highway hypnosis," where you've been driving for miles and you suddenly realize you've been so lost in your thoughts that you've driven to your destination without thinking about the directions at all! This kind of checking out is common for most of us in some form or another, and it all has to do with living more in our minds than our bodies.

Regardless of our geographic location, God gave us one unchanging address for this life on earth, and it is the wondrous body we inhabit. Whether you're happy about it or not, the body that is enabling you to sit wherever you're sitting and to read this right now is the only permanent home you'll have in your life. And some of us spend a lot of our days in just one room of that home—our heads. Of course, we're meant to use these minds of ours for many wonderful things. But it's good to check in with ourselves below the neck sometimes, just to see how "at home" we're feeling in the rest of our bodies!

Reflect

Can you recall a recent experience when you went through the motions of something but later had no recollection of how you did it? Write your experience here.

_____

_____

Pause right now, close your eyes, and take a minute to tune into yourself. Did you find that your awareness is naturally centered in your head? Write about your experience.

_____

_____

Now take a moment to move that awareness down your body intentionally. Are you able to get more of a sense of your whole self? How does it feel?

_____

_____

What are some specific ways each of your senses has helped you to experience the goodness of life today?

_____

_____

What's something simple you could do from time to time to remind yourself to come home to your own body?

_____

_____

Respond

Trying to live with more awareness in such a fast-paced, plugged-in world can feel like swimming upstream sometimes. But if we desire a deeper sense of God's presence, then we need to find ways to become more mindful—more present in ourselves and in the moment. After all, He can't really meet with us if nobody's home when He knocks on the doors of our hearts!

Why not start today, right where you are? Set this book down—maybe even lie down for a few minutes—and take the slowest, deepest breath you can. Feel yourself come back fully to your body. Start from the top of your head and work your way slowly down to your toes, becoming aware of every little part on the way and tuning in to how each part truly feels in this moment. You can even say a prayer of gratitude, thanking your Creator for all that makes you, *you!* This is a practice you can do anytime, anywhere, and the more often you pause during the day just to check in, even for a few moments, the more aware of your whole self you will be.

Remember, God knows the particular reasons that you find yourself in your head sometimes, and He also knows just how to help you come back to the present. If you're feeling like you could use more of that, why not ask Him about it? He may whisper something to your heart through His Word that you hadn't thought of before, or make you aware of a practice you can incorporate into your daily life, or even provide a bit of wisdom through someone you know. Your job is simply to pay attention, be open to guidance, and trust that He will always know how to lead you home.

Challenges are what make life interesting and overcoming them is what makes life meaningful.

JOSHUA MARINE

The Road Ahead

D rawing close to God as we navigate life's challenges may not make the road smoother, but it will always help us to face what's in front of us with more hope, peace, and purpose. Here's a little illustration for you: Imagine a road that's in dire need of repair. Let's say this road runs through a neighborhood and many people take it each day. It's full of potholes, and as you watch the traffic drive over it, you see lots of swerving happening—frustrated drivers trying to navigate the obstacles without causing damage to their cars.

There are three kinds of people you might find driving through that neighborhood: (1) Those who complain every day about the road conditions. They wonder, *When is someone finally going to do something?* (2) Those who just plow through and do their best to ignore it. After all, ignorance is bliss—*right?* (3) Those who decide to take some action. They call the transportation department with their specific concerns, trusting that the help they need will come.

These are the ways that many of us approach life's challenges. Some of us ask why a lot. We're frustrated with the way things are, and we wonder when someone else will fix the problem. Other people just don't want to acknowledge the things that clearly need to be addressed. Maybe we're stretched too thin already, and we simply don't have the energy to deal with the challenges we face. And finally, there are those of us who are ready to face those obstacles head-on and make changes. We've learned that complaining just brings us down and denying doesn't make anything go away. We've decided (possibly after learning the hard way) to call for help this time around—to lean into God and let Him lead us through.

Reflect

What are a few challenges you're facing in your life today?

_____

_____

How are you experiencing those challenges? In what ways do you identify
with any of the approaches described above?

_____

_____

What is one thing you'd like to change about the way you navigate the challenges in your life?

_____

_____

Can you recall a time when you sought God's guidance in difficult circumstances?
What do you feel you learned?

_____

_____

What are some of God's promises about guiding and giving us strength in tough times?
Write them here.

_____

_____

Respond

Notice the way different people around you respond to life's challenges. They can often be mirrors for us, showing us what is hard to see in ourselves. When we catch ourselves thinking, *Wow, I'd never want to act that way*, we can make a note of it. We may find ourselves doing the same thing in the future, and we can remember that it isn't how we want to respond.

On the flip side, when we admire someone's ability to navigate the tough stuff with strength and grace, we can make a note of that too! In fact, if there's someone in your life who seems to walk closely with God through difficulty, consider calling them or making a coffee date with them. Ask about their life and how they've learned to lean on Him. It's likely been quite a process, and they probably have some great wisdom to share. We never know when that kind of wisdom will come in handy. After all, if there's one thing that's true about potholes in life, it's that we rarely see them coming. Even if we're driving a familiar road, it's impossible to avoid *every* bump along the way. Let's give ourselves grace when we're blindsided and have resources ready to help ourselves through.

Most importantly, our Maker sees our challenges coming way before we do. In fact, let's never forget this beautiful truth: He already knows how He's going to use the potholes in our lives for our good—to help us grow and even bless us in ways we can't imagine. His Word is full of promises to provide everything we need on the journey, and the more we fill our hearts with those promises today, the greater our peace will be in the midst of whatever we face tomorrow.

There's nothing more inspiring than the complexity and beauty of the human heart.

CYNTHIA HAND

All That You Are

Do you ever get down on yourself about something you are struggling with and can't seem to overcome? If so, think about this for a moment: Your life is not made of only one ingredient. You are a whole person, full of beautiful complexity. In other words, *you are a whole recipe!* If you are focusing on one glaring thing that frustrates you about yourself at the moment, remember— that's only the tiniest fraction of who you are. There's a whole lot more that makes you, *you!*

The recipe of your life includes some wonderful ingredients but also some things you may still be healing from. As we all know, this life journey contains a little bit of everything. Just think about all that's mixed into your current situation: the place you live and the time you live in, the experiences you've had, and your unique, God-created, biological makeup. And what about your relationships? Consider how others have poured into your life in a positive way and also hurt you at times when you may have been most vulnerable. These are all things that have shaped who you are today. So, if you find yourself feeling discouraged about your progress in any way, just remember: you're dealing with a whole lot more than you probably realize, and you're doing the best you can!

Jesus loved to remind people of the depth of their lives—of the hidden things and all that was happening beneath the surface that they were unaware of. That's part of what God seems to be doing with all of us. He reminds us of everything we are and of the role that each of those things play in our growth toward wholeness in Him.

Reflect

What is one negative thought about yourself that you tend to focus on?

_____

_____

What is one positive thing about yourself that you can start appreciating more?

_____

_____

What repeating patterns in your life do you feel frustrated about sometimes and would like to change?

_____

_____

Is there one small step you could take today toward that change? What is it?

_____

_____

When you witness a loved one struggling with what they feel is a shortcoming, how do you feel toward them? And how does that compare to the way you react to your own struggles?

_____

_____

Respond

Here's an interesting creative exercise that can be both revealing and helpful, if you want to give it a try. Grab some paper or your journal and write "My Recipe" at the top. Then, think about all the things that went into making you who you are today. Make a list of those things, or just write a little freehand reflection on whatever comes to you. It may include the environment you were raised in, your family dynamic, or a few significant things that happened in your growing-up years that left their mark on your life somehow. It might be some of the achievements that have given you confidence, an illness you've struggled through, your career experience, your friendships, or your observations about your personality.

There are no rules about how to do this, so just open your mind and heart! Ask God to reveal things you may not have considered that affect your life today—both positively and negatively. The whole purpose of this exercise is to have a greater appreciation of your depth and complexity as a divinely created human being on this marvelous journey called life.

When you're having a rough day and you're tempted to focus on the parts of yourself that you wish to change, or you're beating yourself up about patterns you can't seem to stop repeating, take a moment and remember that you are like a complex recipe. Remember that who you are today is far more than you are able to see. And most importantly, your Maker sees it all—every facet and layer, every struggle and strength. Hear Him say to your heart: *I know exactly who you are, and I love you.*

The only people who will
get upset about you
setting boundaries
are the ones who benefited
from you having none.

ANONYMOUS

You Can Say No

And now, an important announcement about protecting yourself in this great, big world: *It's a good and healthy thing to have boundaries, and you never have to apologize for them.* Some of us had the blessing of growing up with that understanding. Our caregivers allowed (and maybe even encouraged) us to set our own limits and say no to people or situations that made us uncomfortable. They helped us learn to listen to our God-given intuition, to speak honestly, and to ask for what we needed. And whether that need was a little personal space at home or some distance from a stressful situation, we knew we could depend on our caretakers to honor our boundaries, which brought us a sense of safety and security.

Others of us, however, knew little about personal space when we were young. And that's probably because those who were raising us didn't understand the importance of it either! They couldn't pass along to us what they, themselves, had never received as children. Many people in the generations before us were taught that showing kindness was more important than anything—even if that meant betraying themselves by doing something they knew wasn't right for them.

As adults, we may still be learning how to navigate relationships and learning to commit to loving others while protecting and providing for ourselves. All we have to do is look at Jesus' life to see a perfect example of this. He shared God's love freely, but He also honored His own needs and had no problem saying, "Guys, it's time for me to step away for a bit and recharge."

Reflect

Have you mastered how to set healthy boundaries, or do you feel like you're still learning how to set boundaries? Explain here.

Are there any areas of your life where you feel you've compromised yourself to an unhealthy degree? What are these areas, and how can you work on setting boundaries in them?

Do you often say yes to things when you really mean no? If so, why do you think that's a pattern in your life?

Can you recall a few significant past experiences of setting boundaries with others? How did those boundaries protect you or others?

Who in your life seems to have good balance in this area? What have you observed about them, and how can you learn from their example?

Respond

Think of the dynamics in your relationships for a moment. First, consider your inner circle and how you interact with each person who is close to you. Are there some who tend to drain you? Are there others who may be compromising *themselves* because they're afraid to be honest with you about their needs? And what about your acquaintances—your coworkers or others who touch your life in some way? Do you feel like you're able to say no when you need to, or do you try to be a yes person at all costs? And on the flip side, do you feel like you're respectful of *their* limits and needs?

Try paying close attention to your interactions in the coming days and weeks. This may help you discover some opportunities to strengthen your relationships by opening the door to more honest communication. The Bible reminds us that the more we live in the light of truth, the more our lives will flourish in every area. When we "speak the truth in love" (Ephesians 4:15 NLT), it may be uncomfortable at times, but we can surrender the outcome to God and rest knowing that our job is simply to be obedient.

Some people will naturally feel rejected by our boundaries because they haven't had a lot of experience with them—but that's okay! All we can do is communicate our needs to others in the most loving way possible. Maybe it'll inspire others to do the same for themselves down the road. Remember: Jesus is our model for balance. He is intimately familiar with the pull between loving and caring for others and making sure our human needs are met. Anytime we feel that tension, let's ask for the reassurance and guidance that only He can give.

Time doesn't heal all wounds,
but Jesus does.

ANONYMOUS

Healing Memories

The parts of you that need comfort and reassurance in your life today may feel very young and vulnerable—and that's because they've likely been with you for a long time! This can be true for all of us. Think about it. When we were kids, we sometimes felt fearful and powerless. It's a great, big world we're born into, and when we're just starting out, it can feel pretty overwhelming. At some point, we all had things happen in our lives that we had no control over. Maybe we experienced some kind of sudden crisis, someone's harsh words or actions toward us, or a significant decision we had no say in that affected our future in a big way. We may have felt frightened in those moments—especially if we weren't offered the assurance we needed to know that it was all going to be okay. The adults we are today often carry those young parts of us inside, and when things happen that bring those early, painful memories to the surface, we can suddenly feel defenseless again.

One way we can help ourselves to heal is by revisiting those significant events that left their marks on our memory. We can close our eyes and envision ourselves there, but this time, we can ask Jesus to show us how He has always been with us, even before we knew His name. We might see Him holding us or sense His Spirit comforting us. Whatever our hearts needed in those moments, He knew. He never left our side, even if we didn't realize it back then. And the more we can remind our younger selves of that beautiful truth, the more our grown-up selves can feel it when we face those things that threaten to rock our world—or even just our boats.

Reflect

Can you recall an event from your past that left you feeling vulnerable, afraid, or alone? Describe it here and how you coped with it.

_____

_____

How might you imagine Jesus in that scene with you?

_____

_____

Think of the situations that tend to trigger you today. Could any of them be connected with your younger years? How so?

_____

_____

Can you think of some comforting ways to remind yourself of God's presence when you're feeling particularly vulnerable?

_____

_____

Is there anyone in your life whose struggles may be deeply rooted in their past? How might you offer them compassion and encouragement?

_____

_____

Respond

If you're up for it and want to reflect a bit more on the effect your past may have on you, why not do a little digging? Talk with your family members or lifelong friends about your childhood. See if they have anything to add to your memories. Often, just talking through your younger experiences now that you're an adult will help you to see them with a new perspective.

And when you *do* discover things from your early life that made their marks, consider writing a letter to your younger self about them. Fill it with the compassion, encouragement, and reassurance that you've received from God throughout the years. Tell your past self everything you needed to hear in those moments when you felt most alone and afraid.

And as you observe the people around you, remember that they, too, have a younger self inside, and sometimes those things they do as adults come from old wounds that are still healing. You can choose to be the one who holds a grace-filled space for them, trusting that God is working in them just as He is working in you.

We all grow up and change, but our loving Creator remains the same "yesterday, today, and forever" (Hebrews 13:8 NLT), and that means no matter what the entire span of our lifetime holds, He is right there in it with us—in more ways than we can imagine.

We live within and beyond
our own skin at the same time.

BONNIE BADENOCH

Apart + Together

There are many ways for us to find greater balance in our lives when we're feeling a little unsteady. A really important method is looking at the tension we are experiencing between solitude and connection. We humans are complex creatures, designed to thrive both independently and in community, but never one without the other. And because each of us tends to lean a little more in one of those two directions, it's good to remind ourselves from time to time that we truly do need both!

Some people are born with a need for more space and freedom. They're "do-it-yourselfers." They may not be big on making lots of plans with others, and if they're facing a challenge, they're more likely to try and figure it out alone than to reach out for help. At the other end of the spectrum are those who are natural team players. They're the "includers." They feel a strong need to always cooperate with other people. If they're headed out for a movie, they'll probably invite you! They work well in groups, and they likely have a long list of people to call when they need to talk something through.

No matter which way we lean, the life that God calls us into is a beautiful balance of both. He helps us become strong individuals—nurturing within us the courage, strength, and confidence to stand on our own and be the unique selves He created. But He *also* cultivates the relational part of us, having clearly designed us to support one another in this life. His kingdom is all about *interdependence*—a thriving community made up of one-of-a-kind souls who are learning to care both for themselves and one another.

Reflect

Do you tend more toward independence or community in your life—or both?
Why do you think this is so?

_____

_____

Wherever you are on the scale of connection described above, are there times you've felt
out of balance and wanted to lean a little more in the other direction?
Which direction do you hope to grow in?

_____

_____

Is there a small step you might take toward that balance in the coming days? Write about it here.

_____

_____

Who in your life seems to live with a healthy sense of interdependence,
and what have you observed about them?

_____

_____

When someone talks about the kingdom of God, what kind of life do you imagine?

_____

_____

As we seek to create more balance between solitude and connection in our lives, let's always remember that we are doing the best we can with what we have. We're all wired differently, and it's likely we've been doing life a certain way for a long time! But we can always take small steps toward the interdependence we're truly made for, and as we do, it's likely we'll experience immense joy on the journey.

Think about the last month or so. Did you find yourself at either extreme? Were you primarily isolating yourself and trying to do life mostly on your own? Or were you mostly depending on your connections with others for support, maybe even avoiding alone time as much as possible?

Regardless of where you are in that mix, if you're looking for greater balance, it can help to reflect first on why you have your particular preferences to begin with. Interview yourself with questions like these: What do I most enjoy about being alone or being with others? What brings me anxiety about being alone or being with others? When did I first start to navigate my life this way? Has it changed much over time, and if so, why? How does living at either extreme affect my ability to experience the full life God intends for me? After thinking about your answers, surrender it all to God in prayer. Trust that He will bring you the opportunities you need in order to grow in new directions, and then notice what shows up in the days to come.

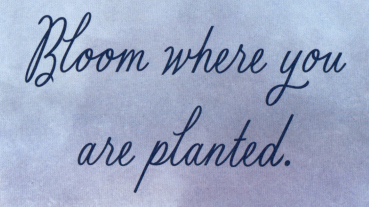

Bloom where you are planted.

MARY ENGLEBREIT

Taking It All In

Take a moment to look around you right now, whether you're indoors or outdoors, alone in a small room or sitting among many other people. How do your surroundings make you feel? Cozy? Peaceful? Anxious? Restless? Whether you're conscious of it or not, your environment is playing a part in your experience of life at every given moment. God gave you a miraculous body with amazing senses that allow you to interact with the creation that surrounds you every day—whether that be people, places, or things. You are a sensory being, and that makes your environment vitally important because you'll always be connected to it in some way.

The truth is, we can't always choose the space we want to be in. We may be stuffed in a cubicle, surrounded by laundry, or dealing with certain people who are part of our everyday lives and we have a hard time being around. But we *can* do our best to work with what we have. During those times when we can't change locations, we can make small adjustments (both without and within) that nudge us toward a more positive experience.

Becoming more aware of how our surroundings affect us is a great first step. Some of the negativity we experience in our days can have a much simpler source than we realize: it may be coming from how we feel about our atmosphere. Discovering this truth can be helpful, especially when we realize that some things are in our power to change.

Reflect

What are your daily environments like, and how do they make you feel?

_____

_____

Who do you share your daily environments with, and what kind of energy do they bring into your life?

_____

_____

Would you consider yourself fairly sensitive to your surroundings, or are you able to tune things out more easily than other people? Explain.

_____

_____

Use your imagination. If you could choose any place to spend a whole day—a place where you would feel a deep sense of joy and contentment—what would it be like?

_____

_____

Are there any elements of the atmosphere you described above that could become part of your daily experience, even in some very small way?

_____

_____

Respond

Even if you spend most of your time in an environment you enjoy, there are usually little things that will bug you about it at some point. And as you've probably noticed, when you put off those little things, they can start feeling like a bigger deal than they need to! Maybe it's sorting one of those piles you've been ignoring, or finally picking out that new paint color, or washing the window—do whatever it is that will help to bring you a greater sense of peace in your space. If you share that space with others, it can be a good exercise to sit down together and talk about how each person feels in your surroundings. What are everyone's favorite things? Who has creative ideas for making changes?

And if your daily environment *isn't* ideal, just take a good look around. As you notice the things you *don't* have control over, be sure and identify the things you *do* have control over. Sometimes when we feel stuck in particular circumstances, we forget that there are small ways we can help ourselves to experience more contentment in the midst of it all. How can you add a few elements that make you smile, help you relax, or remind you to look for the blessings in your days? Maybe a plant or two if you're a nature lover, a photo of your favorite beach, or a Bible verse print that brings peace to your heart. If there's a difficult person you encounter daily, ask God for help in that relationship. Set any boundaries you feel are necessary to avoid being drained by your interactions.

The bottom line is this: Never underestimate the effect your environment has on your well-being, and always remember that the small changes you make can work together to make a big difference in the way you experience your daily life.

All the assumptions
in the world
cannot replace one
single bit of truth.

ANONYMOUS

What We Think We Know

Would you describe yourself as someone who's an open book, or do you tend to be more private about your life? Many of us fall in a different place on that spectrum on any given day, depending on the circumstances and who we're with.

Regardless, we can be sure of one thing: no one except our Maker knows every little thing about us, no matter how "open" we think we are! And of course, we don't know every little thing about anyone *else*—not even our bestie, or our spouse, or that sibling whose sentences we can pretty much finish. It's important for us to remember that when we're dealing with our opinions about others' lives and their opinions about our lives.

No one knows what it's like to live in another person's skin, but sometimes the assumptions we make about one another suggest otherwise. We may witness someone's words or actions and jump to a conclusion that isn't true. That's called misjudgment. And as we have surely noted, Jesus calls us away from judging others—regardless of whether our speculation can be confirmed. His example reminds us that no one is worthy to "throw a stone" (John 8:7) in any situation. Condemning others is simply not our job! And the more we embody this truth, the more peace we'll have inside. We will rest in the fact that He's the only one who sees everything from every angle, and it's His perspective that matters in the end.

Reflect

Can you recall an experience when you made a judgment about someone that was untrue? What happened?

_____

_____

How about a time when someone else misjudged you? How did it make you feel?

_____

_____

What's one thing you wish people understood about you? How can you share this part of yourself with others?

_____

_____

How do you imagine it would have felt to be in the grace-filled presence of Jesus when He was on the earth?

_____

_____

Is there someone in your life whom you appreciate for embodying God's grace and giving others the benefit of the doubt? Have you ever thought of telling them so?

_____

_____

Respond

The small snapshots of life that we see are so limited, but the big picture God sees holds everything. It's good to remember that when we are tempted to assume something about another person and when we are the ones feeling misunderstood. Whether or not we have the chance to fully explain ourselves or clear the air, we can always lean into the comforting truth that God knows us intimately and has a purpose for every situation He allows us to experience.

Are we willing to take an honest look at the kinds of judgments we tend to make about other people? The truth is we may be so used to making them, we don't even realize it's happening much of the time! Just paying attention to those thoughts when they come up is a positive step toward change. And then we can start to choose different ones—more grace-filled and compassionate thoughts. We can ask questions like these: Is that guy at the register grouchy because he's a terrible human, or is he going through a hard time? Is the girl who honked behind me at that red light ridiculously impatient, or is she afraid of being late somewhere important? Did my friend really mean to hurt my feelings, or did her words just come out wrong?

What about choosing a simple phrase to recall when you catch yourself making assumptions? Maybe it's something like this: *There's more to this story than what I can see.* And when the tables are turned and someone is jumping to conclusions about you, try responding this way: *There's more to my story, and I trust that God sees the big picture!* James 2:13 reminds us of the oft-forgotten truth that "mercy triumphs over judgment." Be someone who stands on that truth in your life and watch how it inspires others to do the same.

God speaks in the silence of the heart. Listening is the beginning of prayer.

MOTHER TERESA

How to Be Still

"Be still, and know that I am God" (Psalm 46:10 NIV) is a beloved and well-known verse for good reason. It calms us and reminds us that God is never asking us to perform for Him or try to be more than we are. He's simply calling us to be still and remember who He is to us. This simple truth can set the tone for everything else in our lives. But it's easy to forget that the *knowing* part of that verse comes only *after* the *being still* part. First, we are invited to enter stillness. Only then can we "know" as we become deeply aware of His comforting presence. And for this to happen, we have to do something that can be challenging for many of us: we have to step away from all our doing and spend some intentional time simply *being*.

If you've ever tried practicing stillness—whether to pray and hear from God or to reflect on His Word—you may have learned that it can be really tough to stop and pause. It's hard for many of us to sit with ourselves and our thoughts for very long. Once we turn off the screens and other distractions around us and still our bodies, we become keenly aware of how often our minds overthink and how our thought cycles and obsessions function like a hamster on a wheel. Many of us can only take a few minutes of that total stillness and silence before we reach for something to distract us. Learning to be present in the moment is an exercise for the spirit, just as a workout is for the physical body. We may have to ease into it to build those inner muscles, but the longer we are able to settle into that simple awareness, the more of God's wonderful peace we can feel.

Reflect

Do you lean toward introversion or extroversion, or both?
How do you think it has affected your spiritual life?

_____

_____

Does the idea of sitting alone with your thoughts give you a feeling of unease,
or do you welcome that stillness and shift into it more naturally? Explain here.

_____

_____

When you do find time alone, without distraction, are there particular thoughts that you notice
rising up and calling for your attention? What are they?

_____

_____

Can you recall a time of being still that brought you a great sense of peace
or awareness of God's presence? Write about it here.

_____

_____

Can you think of a regular time in your day or week that you might set aside even ten minutes
with the intention of sitting quietly? When and where?

_____

_____

Respond

Consider setting aside a few minutes today, or in the near future, to quietly sit and just *be* in God's presence. See what happens. If your mind starts to chatter—which tends to happen for most of us—try watching whatever appears as an observer might. Imagine a stream or a breeze, or whatever comes to mind, as something that could move those thoughts along and out of your sight. Just watch them flow away and trust that anything needing attention will be resolved in God's time. Right now, your intention is to let everything else go in order to make space for your simple awareness of Him.

As your mind naturally wanders, don't judge it or overly exert yourself to rein it in. Just take a deep breath and simply come back to where you're sitting. Again and again. Sense God's quiet presence with you. Understand that He is delighting in your company, just as you delight in His. You may even feel it in your heart to smile and soak in the warmth of His loving gaze. For some people, it helps to have a phrase or short verse to say, just to help them focus. These can be very simple thoughts like, *Thank You, Jesus*, which lifts our hearts in gratitude, and, *God's peace is with me*, which reminds us of the very real connection we share with Him.

In the beginning, these times of quiet may be short, but they can still be powerful moments shared with the heart of your Creator. Never underestimate the benefit that comes from even a brief time of being still and knowing Him.

*Your worth
and peoples approval
are two different things.
Learn to separate the two.*

BRITTNEY MOSES

Always Worthy

How you're feeling about your life today is affected in some way (whether you realize it or not) by your sense of self-worth. The stronger that sense of worth becomes within you, the more confidence you live with. And the more of that confidence you build, the less you will be derailed by the opinions and judgments of those around you.

One way we can tell just how grounded we are in who God created us to be is by observing what happens when others claim to be disappointed by us. Whether it's an acquaintance, a coworker, or someone in our inner circle, it can be really painful when they look at us with a face that says, "You dropped the ball." But guess what? As hard as we try, we will all fall short sometimes. Before we allow ourselves to fall into the rabbit hole of thinking, *I'm not good enough* or *I'll never get it right*, it's important to consider the details of whatever disappointing thing just happened. Sure, it may simply be that we messed something up unintentionally—we forgot an important event, didn't finish something on time, or weren't available when someone needed us. These things happen because we are human beings managing complex lives in a busy world. We aren't setting out to intentionally hurt anyone. We're just doing the best we can with what we have.

Sometimes, though, it isn't about us at all. Sometimes, others are disappointed in us because of their unrealistic expectations. We can find great comfort in remembering this. Even if someone points a finger at us, it's not a burden we need to bear. They may have set the bar impossibly high and expected us to deliver beyond our ability. Or, maybe they have a hard time admitting that *they're* the ones who missed the mark, so they try to make it about someone else instead. Regardless of what anyone claims, our Creator is the only one who can truly understand our motives. He calls us to draw close in times like these so that He might speak the truth to our hearts and offer the assurance and guidance that only He can give.

Reflect

When was the last time you felt like you let someone down, and how did you deal with it?

_____

_____

How often do you find yourself feeling disappointed with others, and how do you handle it?

_____

_____

Can you recall a time when someone held you responsible for something that wasn't your fault? How did you respond?

_____

_____

Look up Galatians 1:10 and ask yourself, "Where in my life do I rely most heavily on the approval of others?"

_____

_____

What is one small way you can remind yourself regularly that your worth is not based on your performance or on others' perceptions of you?

_____

_____

If we want to live with less fear about "messing up" in our lives, it all starts with laying a solid foundation of sacred self-worth—standing on the truth of who God says we are. No matter how many balls we drop or what anyone else says or thinks about us, this is where we can always find firm footing.

What about finding a few "love notes" that God has written to us in His Word and keeping them close? After you've selected some verses that describe God's love for you, consider making a list of the things that *you* love about yourself. This can be tough for a lot of us to do, but it's vital to see the good in ourselves, especially when our perceived shortcomings have taken center stage. Ask yourself things like, "What natural gifts has God given me, and how am I using them? What are some unique things about myself that make me smile? How do I bring joy to those around me daily?"

Next time you find yourself in a disappointing situation, stop for a moment and ask yourself: "What's really going on?" If there are amends to be made, ask God for the courage and grace to make them and move on, trusting that God sees your heart and never withdraws an ounce of His love, no matter how anyone else feels about you. If you believe that someone has held you to an impossible standard—and maybe it's more about them than you—be honest and tell them so. And just remember: in the end, no matter what happens, or how, or with whom . . . you can trust that God sees your intentions. He is always working to bring about the greatest good for you and everyone involved because we all have infinite worth in His eyes.

If you don't like something, change it. If you can't change it, change your attitude.

MAYA ANGELOU

Silver Linings

God always gives us a choice when we feel disappointment or discouragement creeping up—we can resent the situation that brought it about and allow it to drag us down or we can accept what is and let it be a stepping-stone toward something greater.

We've all had some disheartening times—whether it be work stresses, raising children, financial uncertainty, or even the opportunities we once had that are no longer available. On one hand, we may experience some of these changes as positive ones. Maybe we needed a little wake-up call to do some things differently in life.

But on the other hand, we may feel like the life we're living now isn't how we wanted it to be at all. We had plans that were derailed and ideas that couldn't become realities. It's natural to feel the deep disappointment of unfulfilled dreams. The pull toward *what might have been* can be really strong when we haven't yet found peace with *what is.*

To be clear, accepting where we are today doesn't mean settling or giving up. It doesn't mean not hoping for more or not pursuing the dreams we know God has hidden within us. Acceptance is just that moment of looking around and saying from our hearts, "This is my life right now, and I'm trusting that God knows exactly what He's up to." It's where we find our solid footing in reality before we take that first step on the next leg of the journey. It's where we meet Him in the "now" of our lives and say, "I'm okay with my present circumstances, and I'm trusting You to guide me into what's next."

Reflect

Do you feel like you are someone who tends to go with the flow when you're facing change, or do you have a hard time adjusting? Explain below.

_____

_____

What kinds of adjustments have you had to make in your life recently, and how have you felt about them?

_____

_____

What things about your current life situation do you wish you had a more positive attitude about?

_____

_____

Do you find yourself drawing closer to God and leaning into Him in times of uncertainty? If so, how?

_____

_____

What's one thing you can be grateful for in your life right now?

_____

_____

Centuries after Paul reminded us to "give thanks in all circumstances" (I Thessalonians 5:18 NIV), gratitude is still recognized as one of the main pillars of a happy life. And those times when we find ourselves feeling frustrated and ungrateful are the times that can transform us beautifully. The low points in our lives can be like red flags reminding us that we need to shift our focus from our lack to our abundance. We've all heard that our disappointment is never truly about what's happening to us. It's about how we choose to *see* what's happening. And that's always in our power.

Set aside a few minutes in your day to make a list of the things that you wish were different in your life right now. It might be a commute to work, a spirit-squashing neighbor who loves to rain on your parade, a health issue, or a financial burden. Just get it all out so you can tell yourself the truth about it.

Talk to God about your frustrations. Be honest about the changes you're hoping for, but also ask for the grace to accept what *is*—just as it is—today. Ask for help to make any changes that are possible for you so that you can experience more inner peace in those situations.

Then, make one more list of things you are grateful for about the life you're living right here, right now. That will be your "silver linings" list. If you make it a regular practice to look for blessings every day, you'll be surprised at how much brighter the world gets—not because your circumstances change, but because your perspective does.

Integrity gives you real freedom because you have nothing to fear since you have nothing to hide.

ZIG ZIGLAR

Inside Out

Here's an important connection you may have noticed in your life: the more integrity you choose to live with, the more peace you get to enjoy. How have you seen this play out, and what does it look like for you right now?

Consider this definition of *integrity*: *The state of being whole and undivided.* That means it's more than just a moral standard—more than our actions aligning with our words. It's also living in a way that our inside matches our outside. The words we speak are *revealing* and not *hiding* the truth we carry within. When we open our mouths, are we doing so with honesty, or are we telling people what they want to hear? Are we flattering with our tongues but resenting with our hearts? Are we using words to circumnavigate the hard things that God may be calling us to walk through in our relationships?

Anytime we lean toward "faking it" in any way, we take on the burden of managing a facade, and that can drain our sense of peace in a big way. When we find ourselves praying for a calmer spirit in our daily lives, we need to remember that a calm spirit is the fruit of an integrated life. We weren't designed to live with division within, and when we do, it can cause a lot of stress and anxiety. We were created to thrive as whole beings, like Jesus did, and that means learning more and more to "speak the truth in love" (Ephesians 4:15 NLT). The more our lives flow with integrity, the less friction we'll experience between the true and the false and the less energy we'll spend trying to fill the gap between who we really are on the inside and who we're pretending to be on the outside. Our relationships will become more authentic because there's less and less to hide.

Reflect

Would you say you are more vocal or more reserved when it comes to communicating? Why?

_____

_____

When was the last time you remember experiencing friction between what you were expressing on the outside and what you were feeling on the inside?

_____

_____

Who in your life would you point to as an example of someone who lives with integrity?

_____

_____

Do you sense a gap between what you're sharing with the world and what you're feeling inside, or do you feel more of a natural flow between your inner and outer life?

_____

_____

Can you find a biblical example of living with integrity and an example of the consequences of living without it?

_____

_____

Respond

You've probably heard the saying, "If you can't say anything nice, don't say anything at all." But if you replace the word *nice* with *truthful* and read it again, that phrase really gets to the heart of the matter. It's not about saying *nice* things in order to spare someone's feelings; it's about sharing honest words (even if it takes courage to speak them) in order to help bring about God's highest good for everyone. The more we practice this kind of authentic, intentional communication, the more naturally it will become a part of our daily experience.

We can start by considering how we tend to use our words. Try asking yourself these questions: How often do I speak just to fill the silence? How often do I say what I think other people want to hear instead of being honest about my feelings? Am I able to relax and enjoy most conversations with others, or do I have a sense of anxiety about expressing myself? When I think of my most significant relationships, how clear and direct is the communication? Do I have any connections that feel one-sided when it comes to expressing our feelings and needs?

Only you know how truthfully you're showing up in the world, because while others can see the image you project, no one else but you (and your Maker) knows what is happening in that heart of yours. One thing is certain: you're a work in progress. We all are! Even if today you feel more limited in your self-expression, God is always inviting you to take steps toward greater integrity. He knows that the more authentically you show up in your life, the greater sense of peace and freedom you will live with. And just like any loving earthly father, He wants to see you live the fullest, freest life imaginable.

In any given moment,
we have two options:
to step forward into growth
or step back into safety.

ABRAHAM MASLOW

Our Only Constant

Have you ever watched kids on a merry-go-round or other amusement park rides? The moment things start moving, everyone reaches for something to hold on to. We humans (big and small) have that tendency—a natural instinct to steady ourselves when we're thrown off balance unexpectedly.

This is what happens when we face change or uncertainty in our lives. We often look for something or someone to hold on to—to calm and reassure us, and to remind us that we are safe, even if things feel a bit chaotic at the moment. As we all know, this will likely happen more than once on this unpredictable path we call "life." Because, given enough time, everything changes: our relationships, our circumstances, our perspectives, even our spiritual journeys. And change can be amazing, but it can also be quite disorienting and maybe even a little (or a lot!) scary at first.

It's been said that the only constant in life is change, but if we really think about it, we know that's not true. Because there's another, even *more constant*, constant! And it's not a thing; it's our God. The One "who is, and who was, and who is to come" (Revelation 1:8 NIV). The still point in our lives that we can always return to when we need to find sure footing again. Trusting God's love and sovereignty over every other thing that comes our way can completely transform our experience of life's transitions. Instead of digging in our heels, trying to cling to the old and resist the new, or even resenting whatever is happening to us, we can learn to embrace it. We can focus more and more on what our heavenly Father is doing through it all—how He's guiding us, helping us grow, protecting us, and offering us His peace along the way.

Reflect

What's the biggest change you've been through recently, and what was the experience like for you?

----

*Do you tend to find comfort in routine, thrive in spontaneity,
or feel like you have a pretty good balance of both? Explain.*

----

*Is there any kind of change or transition (large or small) that you're facing in your life right now?
Write about it here.*

What are some ways your faith can help you navigate through that transition?

----

*What's one thing you could do today to help remind you of God's constant presence
in whatever you may face tomorrow?*

Respond

One place where we can witness the beauty and purpose of transformation is in nature. When you find yourself feeling a sense of doubt or uncertainty about the changes happening in your life, try spending a little time outdoors. Watch how all of creation ebbs and flows, and how things that fall to the ground and take root just grow again in another form. Just by looking at a seed or a cocoon, it's impossible to guess what magnificent growth and metamorphosis is taking place within. Perhaps that's one reason why many of us are drawn to the great outdoors—creation is one way God reveals truths to us about how all of life works, including our own!

If you're not an outdoorsy sort of person, that's okay! Just take your observations indoors. There's plenty of creation in there too, including the people who surround you! Take time to observe those fellow humans of yours. Watch how their relationships play out and how every day is a new challenge to meet or celebration to experience together. When you're sitting at an airport, or a party, or a family get-together, think about all the dynamics that go into the connections that are happening around you. Showing up for our lives (and for each other) in a constantly changing world is no small thing. Give yourself lots of grace when it comes to all this holding on and letting go. Remember that we all experience the fear of the unknown or unfamiliar at some point. We all walk through times of vulnerability, and we all need reminders that through it all, we can count on the loving, sustaining presence of our Maker.

Lighten up on yourself.
No one is perfect.
Gently accept
your humanness.

DEBORAH DAY

Forgiving You

The Bible reminds us more than a few times about the importance of forgiveness—how it frees the person we've chosen to forgive but also frees *us* from holding a grudge we're not meant to carry; how we imitate God when we take that first step toward reconciliation (no matter how much we want to run in the other direction sometimes); and even how we may be tired of forgiving someone repeatedly, but as Jesus says to Peter in Matthew 18:22, we're called to forgive not "seven times, but seventy-seven times." (In other words, *a whole bunch of times!*)

Here's something to remember when you think about giving grace like that: There's someone you may be forgetting who needs your forgiveness more often than you realize. It's someone who can feel pretty discouraged at times, who is well aware that they aren't perfect but who needs unconditional love and compassion just like everybody else. And guess what? That someone is *you*.

Forgiving ourselves can be tricky because often the resentment we carry within us is hidden, and we're not aware of how it's affecting us. It's not played out through an outward relationship with another person who we feel wronged us. It's the *internal* struggle we feel as the result of something we wish we hadn't done. Some of us have needed to experience reconciliation within for a long time. Because here's the thing: *other* people have forgiven us, we know God *always* forgives us, but if we're still holding something against *ourselves*, it can be hard to fully receive God's grace.

Reflect

Is self-forgiveness something you've thought about before? If so, write about your experience. If not, why not?

_____

_____

When someone forgives you, do you feel the true freedom in it, or do you often revisit the memory of it and feel regretful? Explain here.

_____

_____

When you experience God's grace in your life, do you feel like you resist it, or are you open to receiving it, knowing that it's freely given and impossible to earn? Explain why.

_____

_____

What is one of your earliest memories of "messing up" in some way, and how would you reassure your younger self with words of grace and forgiveness?

_____

_____

Do you know someone who seems to have a hard time forgiving themselves? How might you encourage them next time you notice it happening?

_____

_____

Respond

We hear plenty about the importance of forgiving others, and rightly so. In a culture where many may be quick to condemn and slow to offer compassion, we can shine the light of Christ brightly by giving grace in tough situations. The more freely we receive God's grace for us, the more freely we can extend it to others. But let us always remember that it has to start within ourselves.

So, how about you and your heart? Is there anything unresolved that could use some tender loving care? Try spending a little time in prayer to ask God if there's any shame in your heart that you may not even realize you're carrying. Read the following verses and think about them in the context of self-forgiveness.

- *"Hatred stirs up strife, but love covers all offenses"* (Proverbs 10:12 NASB).

- *"Therefore there is now no condemnation at all for those who are in Christ Jesus"* (Romans 8:1 NASB).

- *"Be kind and compassionate to one another, forgiving each other, just as in Christ God forgave you"* (Ephesians 4:32 NIV).

- *"As far as the east is from the west, so far has He removed our transgressions from us"* (Psalm 103:12 NIV).

Your heavenly Father is surely willing and always able to release you from whatever you might be holding against yourself. Remember: the person looking back at you in the mirror is infinitely precious to Him, and He delights in helping you to let go of anything that holds you back from living more freely in His love.

*Rejoice with your family
in the beautiful land of life!*

ALBERT EINSTEIN

Family Matters

C an we talk about family for a moment? How's it going with yours? The people we call "family" often have a significant impact on the quality of our lives, and it's good to reflect now and then on the strength and health of those specific relationships.

At some point in your life, you probably discovered that there are no "normal" families. Of course, some of us came from what is considered a stable family, and others came from more turbulent backgrounds. Regardless of the environment we grew up in, it is easy to look at the other side of things and make assumptions. For example, it's easy to assume that nice families never have problems or that troubled families produce troubled kids. But the truth is that every small group of people sharing four walls and a roof is going to have lots of different things to work through. Plus, those little groups are connected to other relatives who bring something to the mix. The bottom line is this: *families can be complicated!*

How about you? What kind of life did you have growing up? If you came from a warm and loving home, what a gift! Hopefully, you're able to pass that gift along to your own children or to others who didn't have the blessing of a stable family life. Or maybe you didn't grow up with a sense of safety and belonging. Maybe you struggle with it even today. If that's the case, please know that your heavenly Father desires to provide those loving connections for you. You are part of His eternal family, after all, and you can sense His wonderful assurance throughout your life in many ways.

Reflect

How would you describe your family relationships as you were growing up?

_____

_____

Do you remember looking at families that weren't like yours and making assumptions about them, whether positive or negative? Explain.

_____

_____

What have you learned through the years about what it means to be family?

_____

_____

How's it going today with those you share your life with?
Do you feel like you've been able to prioritize your connections with them?

_____

_____

Who do you feel most and least connected to in your family right now?

_____

_____

Respond

Think about the people you consider to be your family. Whether they live in your home or are scattered around the globe, whether you have the same blood, share a deep friendship, or are brothers and sisters in Christ, those connections are gifts from God, and His Word reminds us of the importance of nurturing them. It's good to remember that when we've asked Him to provide for our needs in the past, our loved ones have often been answers to those prayers!

Try making a list of the most special people in your life, and beside each name write one thing you might do to connect with them more intentionally. It could be something as simple as taking the time for a nightly hug or a weekly text—whatever might communicate how precious they are to you. It's so easy these days to rush past one another, and it takes some commitment to slow down and be present with each other for a few moments. But the positive effect those loving gestures can have on our relationships is greater than we may realize.

And what about your end of things? Do you feel loved and nurtured by those you share your life with? Are there needs *you* have that you haven't expressed? Do you wish you had more close, heart-to-heart connections with others? Ask God to show you how you can more fully experience the lifelong, soul-deep relationships He provides. And remember to lean into Him when you find yourself struggling with the inevitable growing pains that every close relationship brings. He is always there with reassurance, guidance, and grace, offering you a place in His heart to call home.

Honesty is more than not lying. It is truth telling, truth speaking, truth living, and truth loving.

JAMES E. FAUST

To Tell You the Truth

Here's something important to consider when we're going through tough times: God often provides comfort and encouragement through the people around us, but they won't know to share it with us if they don't realize how much we need it. And that requires us to be honest about how we feel, especially on our hard days. Think about it. When you say, "How are you?" to other people, do you notice how often they give an automatic, "I'm fine," response? Sometimes, people truly are doing fine. They're living their best lives and have no complaints. But other times, you might catch a glimpse of something in their eyes that suggests otherwise. You can tell that no matter what they're about to say, they're not really *fine*. And once in a blue moon, you'll even hear an *honest* answer from someone, like, "You know what? I'm not doing so well today."

How about you? When someone asks you about yourself, do you have an automatic response prepared? Do you ever wish you could just say how you *really* feel on rough days? And if you *did*, do you think it might get awkward? The truth is, it probably would! At least for a moment or two. And that's because giving a real, from-the-heart answer requires more than small talk, and a lot of us would rather keep it on the surface. Those autopilot conversations feel comfortable and safe, and most of us are so used to them, we don't even think about what we're saying!

But we always have an opportunity during those encounters to offer a little more of ourselves. In fact, doing so can not only open the door for others to encourage us but also inspire them to be honest about their own feelings when they are the ones struggling. And as we all know, everybody struggles sometimes.

Reflect

*Think about what happens when you run into an acquaintance somewhere.
What's your go-to response when someone asks how you are doing?*

_____

_____

*Are you someone who draws others into conversation when you're out and about,
or do you do your best to avoid small talk? Why?*

_____

_____

*Do you remember a time when you or another person opened up unexpectedly in conversation
and where it led? Write about it here.*

_____

_____

If someone asked how you were doing today and you chose to respond honestly, what would you say?

_____

_____

What are a few Bible verses that speak about the importance of honest communication?

_____

_____

Respond

We often encounter people who have something they need to express, but they're holding it in. They may feel that no one has the time to listen, or even if others did listen, they might not understand. You may know what that feels like too. Carrying a burden alone creates a sense of heaviness and loneliness in our lives that we weren't intended to bear.

Allowing ourselves to be vulnerable and truthful with others (when we really want to run and hide) can be a kind of ministry. When we're willing to crack the door open into our lives and let others see inside, we might inspire them to do the same. When they witness the humility that it takes to admit that we don't have it all together, they may find the courage to let their guard down too.

Start paying close attention to the automatic responses people give in conversations. Look into their eyes. Get a sense of their sincerity. Next time someone answers "fine" to your "How are you?" and you can clearly see that they're *not* fine, consider taking a moment to press in and say, "Are you *sure*?" See if they might have more to share. It doesn't have to turn into an hour-long conversation. It may just be a few moments of much-needed connection, an offer of a hug, or even a promise to pray for them. We never know what a difference a small gesture can make. And when the tables are turned, let's try and keep ourselves open to the support that others offer us too. The more openly and honestly we live, the more space we make for the comfort and encouragement God sends our way through those who touch our lives.

For Jesus doesn't change—yesterday, today, tomorrow, He's always totally Himself.

HEBREWS 13:8 THE MESSAGE

The Send-Off

"I am Alpha and Omega, the beginning and the end, the first and the last" (Revelation 22:13 KJV). What could comfort us more than these words of Jesus, which are filled with all the reassurance we will ever need? His infinite love bookends this life we're living. *Everything* begins and ends in Him. Our very being, our first breath, and our first real steps of faith. Every day of our lives, He is the beginning—the source behind the sunrise, the catalyst for our growth, healing, and wholeness as cherished children of God.

And He is our destination. His open arms and grace-filled heart are where we are always headed. Everything that happens on this journey of life is leading us home to Him. We may feel uncertainty along the way. We may feel beat down by discouragement, confused by doubt, and hindered by fear, but those things will never have the last word. His Word is the last word. The promises we stand on are not wishes or temporary fixes or great ideas for how to get through life a little easier. They are what our faith is made of—"the substance of things hoped for, the evidence of things not seen" (Hebrews 11:1 KJV). The truth of God is the most substantial, reliable, and unchanging force in the universe, and it is available to us daily in His presence, His creation, and His Word. Hold on to that truth tightly when you feel alone or afraid or misunderstood. When you are seeking comfort, know how closely you are being held and guided by the One who loves you more than you can possibly imagine.

Reflect

What are the most significant things you will take away from this forty-day (or longer) journey?

_____

_____

What have you learned about yourself and the loving God who made you?

_____

_____

Are there ways you feel your heart has been lightened, and if so, how?

_____

_____

Are there any specific, significant things you feel God is calling you to do after reading this book? Write them here.

_____

_____

Is there anyone in your life who could use these messages of comfort and encouragement right now?

_____

_____

Respond

Our Creator provides many ways for us to grow in faith, love, and freedom throughout our lives, but we always have the choice about how we'll respond to the lessons and experiences He allows. We can choose to remain stuck in the familiar patterns we may have lived with for a long time, or we can open ourselves to more life-giving ways of being in the world. We can choose to see our challenges as negative experiences to avoid at all costs, or we can embrace whatever comes and allow Him to use our hardships for our healing—just as He intends.

We all know that a calmer spirit doesn't develop in a single, miraculous moment. It is often the result of walking through trials—learning to weather life's storms hand in hand with the One who allows them. The divine comfort we seek can reach us right in the midst of chaos and uncertainty because His comfort doesn't come from our circumstances; it comes from our focus. We must keep our eyes on Jesus, not on the trials we face. His hand is forever outstretched to steady and reassure us. He is not calling us to take a detour or to find an escape from the hard things. He is leading us right through it all. He's asking us to turn our eyes toward Him and to put our trust in Him, every day. And as a result, we will experience the soul-soothing peace and deep joy that can only come from surrendering our lives to the God who knows and loves us best.

The Comfort Promises by

DaySpring

No matter what you are facing today, you can rest in knowing the Creator of the universe loves you. He loves you deeply and perfectly with absolutely no conditions. And He's made hundreds of promises to you!

Below you'll find the 100 most referenced, quoted, and memorized Bible promises. At DaySpring, we call these The Comfort Promises™—the verses we turn to again and again for encouragement, joy, and strength. For your convenience, we've provided a quick reference guide—a unique tool that makes it easy for you to find just the right comfort promises for your immediate need.

When you are afraid . . .

He will not allow your foot to slip;
He who keeps you will not slumber.
PSALM 121:3 NASB

Do not fear; I will help you.
ISAIAH 41:13 NIV

Draw near to God, and He will draw near to you.
JAMES 4:8 CSB

When you are anxious . . .

If you follow Me, you won't have to walk in darkness,
because you will have the light that leads to life.
JOHN 8:12 NLT

Don't fret or worry. Instead of worrying, pray.
PHILIPPIANS 4:6 THE MESSAGE

He never changes or casts a shifting shadow.
JAMES 1:17 NLT

When you need assurance . . .

He is the faithful God, keeping His covenant
of love to a thousand generations.
DEUTERONOMY 7:9 NIV

You're blessed when you're at the end of your rope.
With less of you there is more of God.
MATTHEW 5:3 THE MESSAGE

He chose us...that we would be holy
and blameless before Him.
EPHESIANS 1:4 NASB

You are saved by grace through faith...
it is God's gift.
EPHESIANS 2:8 CSB

He cares about you.
I PETER 5:7 NLT

His divine power has given us
everything required for life.
II PETER 1:3 CSB

When you need comfort . . .

The Lord is near the brokenhearted;
He saves those crushed in spirit.
PSALM 34:18 CSB

Take delight in the Lord,
and He will give you your heart's desires.
PSALM 37:4 CSB

My faithful love for you will remain.
My covenant of blessing will never be broken.
ISAIAH 54:10 NLT

I have it all planned out—plans to take care of you,
not abandon you, plans to give you the future
you hope for.
JEREMIAH 29:11 THE MESSAGE

He will rejoice over you with gladness...
He will delight in you with singing.
ZEPHANIAH 3:17 CSB

Blessed are those who mourn,
for they shall be comforted.
MATTHEW 5:4 ESV

He comforts us in all our troubles
so that we can comfort others.
II CORINTHIANS 1:4 NLT

God has chosen you and made you His holy people.
He loves you.
COLOSSIANS 3:12 ICB

When you need courage . . .

But You, Lord, are a shield around me, my glory,
and the One who lifts up my head.
PSALM 3:3 CSB

I can do all things through Christ
because He gives me strength.
PHILIPPIANS 4:13 ICB

He hears their cry for help and saves them.
PSALM 145:19 CSB

I will strengthen you, I will help you,
I will uphold you with my righteous right hand.
ISAIAH 41:10 ESV

This is what the Lord says, he who made the earth,
the Lord who formed it and established it—the Lord
is His name: "Call to me and I will answer you and tell
you great and unsearchable things you do not know."
JEREMIAH 33:2–3 NIV

The Lord is good to those who wait for Him,
to the person who seeks Him.
LAMENTATIONS 3:25 NASB

I will send you the Helper from the Father.
He is the Spirit of truth who comes from the Father.
JOHN 15:26 ICB

He hears us.
I JOHN 5:14 NASB

When you need hope . . .

The Lord will fight for you while you keep silent.
EXODUS 14:14 NASB

Be strong; don't give up, for your work has a reward.
II CHRONICLES 15:7 CSB

The Lord grants favor and honor;
He does not withhold the good
from those who live with integrity.
PSALM 84:11 CSB

He has planted eternity in the human heart.
ECCLESIASTES 3:11 NLT

His mercies never end.
They are new every morning.
LAMENTATIONS 3:22–23 CSB

I am the living bread....
Whoever eats this bread will live forever.
JOHN 6:51 NIV

Anyone who believes in Me will live,
even after dying.
JOHN 11:25 NLT

We have this hope as an anchor for the soul,
firm and secure.
HEBREWS 6:19 NIV

When you need joy . . .

Do not grieve, for the joy of the Lord is your strength.
NEHEMIAH 8:10 NIV

You will fill me with joy in Your presence.
PSALM 16:11 NIV

You turned my lament into dancing.
PSALM 30:11 CSB

Give, and it will be given to you.
LUKE 6:38 NIV

When you are lonely . . .

He will be with you; He will not leave you
or abandon you.
DEUTERONOMY 31:8 CSB

The Lord your God is with you wherever you go.
JOSHUA 1:9 CSB

He Himself has said,
"I will never leave you or abandon you."
HEBREWS 13:5 CSB

When you are feeling overwhelmed . . .

For nothing will be impossible with God.
LUKE 1:37 ESV

The God of all grace...will himself restore,
confirm, strengthen, and establish you.
I PETER 5:10 ESV

When you need peace . . .

The Lord gives His people strength;
the Lord blesses His people with peace.
PSALM 29:11 CSB

Peace I leave with you. My peace I give to you.
JOHN 14:27 CSB

God's peace will keep your hearts and minds
in Christ Jesus.
PHILIPPIANS 4:7 ICB

When you need protection . . .

You are a hiding place for me;
you preserve me from trouble.
PSALM 32:7 ESV

You protect people as a bird
protects her young under her wings.
PSALM 36:7 ICB

God has not given us a spirit of fear,
but one of power, love, and sound judgment.
II TIMOTHY 1:7 CSB

Humble yourselves before the Lord,
and He will lift you up.
JAMES 4:10 NIV

When you need encouragement . . .

His faithful love endures forever.
PSALM 100:5 CSB

I will be your God throughout your lifetime—
until your hair is white with age.
ISAIAH 46:4 NLT

I will give you a new heart
and put a new spirit within you.
EZEKIEL 36:26 CSB

For I am convinced that neither death nor life,
neither angels nor demons, neither the present
nor the future, nor any powers, neither height
nor depth, nor anything else in all creation,
will be able to separate us from the love of God
that is in Christ Jesus our Lord.
ROMANS 8:38–39 NIV

He will not let you be tempted beyond your ability.
I CORINTHIANS 10:13 ESV

He has created us anew in Christ Jesus,
so we can do the good things He planned for us.
EPHESIANS 2:10 NLT

When you need forgiveness . . .

I will forgive their sin and will heal their land.
II CHRONICLES 7:14 NIV

Though your sins are scarlet,
they will be as white as snow.
ISAIAH 1:18 CSB

By giving Himself completely at the Cross,
actually dying for you, Christ brought you over
to God's side and put your lives together,
whole and holy in His presence.
COLOSSIANS 1:22 THE MESSAGE

He...will forgive us our sins and purify us.
I JOHN 1:9 NIV

God, who...will bring you with great joy
into His glorious presence without a single fault.
JUDE 1:24 NLT

When you need guidance . . .

He will make your paths straight.
PROVERBS 3:6 CSB

The Lord will continually guide you.
ISAIAH 58:11 NASB

When the Spirit of truth comes,
He will guide you into all truth.
JOHN 16:13 NLT

When you need healing . . .

He heals the brokenhearted
and binds up their wounds.
PSALM 147:3 ESV

By His wounds we are healed.
ISAIAH 53:5 NIV

I will give you back your health
and heal your wounds.
JEREMIAH 30:17 NLT

When you need help . . .

I will send you rain in its season, and the ground
will yield its crops and the trees their fruit.
LEVITICUS 26:4 NIV

Day after day He bears our burdens.
PSALM 68:19 CSB

He will give His angels orders...
to protect you in all your ways.
PSALM 91:11 CSB

The Lord will guard your going out and your
coming in from this time forth and forever.
PSALM 121:8 NASB

He is a shield to those who take refuge in Him.
PROVERBS 30:5 CSB

A stronghold for the poor...
a refuge from storms
and a shade from heat.
ISAIAH 25:4 CSB

No weapon turned against you will succeed.
ISAIAH 54:17 NLT

He will strengthen you and protect you.
II THESSALONIANS 3:3 NIV

When you need rest *and* renewal . . .

The Lord is my shepherd, I lack nothing.
He makes me lie down in green pastures,
He leads me beside quiet waters.
PSALM 23:1–2 NIV

He renews my life; He leads me along
the right paths for His name's sake.
PSALM 23:3 CSB

He satisfies you with good things;
your youth is renewed like the eagle.
PSALM 103:5 CSB

Those who wait for the Lord will gain new strength;
they will mount up with wings like eagles,
they will run and not get tired, they will walk
and not become weary.
ISAIAH 40:31 NASB

Come to me, all who labor and are heavy laden,
and I will give you rest.
MATTHEW 11:28 ESV

The Son of Man came to find and restore the lost.
LUKE 19:10 THE MESSAGE

Jesus answered, "Everyone who drinks this water
will be thirsty again, but whoever drinks the water
I give them will never thirst. Indeed, the water
I give them will become in them a spring of water
welling up to eternal life."
JOHN 4:13–14 NIV

Our inner person is being renewed day by day.
II CORINTHIANS 4:16 CSB

If anyone is in Christ, he is a new creation.
II CORINTHIANS 5:17 CSB

When you need strength . . .

He gives power to the weak and strength
to the powerless.
ISAIAH 40:29 NLT

The Spirit helps us in our weakness.
ROMANS 8:26 ESV

He will keep you strong to the end so that
you will be free from all blame on the day
when our Lord Jesus Christ returns.
I CORINTHIANS 1:8 NLT

When you are **suffering** . . .

He will sustain you; He will never allow
the righteous to be shaken.
PSALM 55:22 NASB

As a father has compassion on his children,
so the Lord has compassion on those who fear Him;
for He knows how we are formed,
He remembers that we are dust.
PSALM 103:13–14 NIV

I will be with you...
When you walk through the fire,
you will not be scorched.
ISAIAH 43:2 CSB

The Lord is good, a stronghold in the day of trouble.
NAHUM 1:7 ESV

Remain in Me, and I will remain in you.
JOHN 15:4 NLT

When you need **wisdom** . . .

Continue to ask, and God will give to you.
Continue to search, and you will find.
Continue to knock, and the door will open for you.
MATTHEW 7:7 ICB

It is because of Him that you are in Christ Jesus,
who has become for us wisdom from God—
that is, our righteousness, holiness and redemption.
I CORINTHIANS 1:30 NIV

Now if any of you lacks wisdom, he should ask God...
and it will be given to him.
JAMES 1:5 CSB

When you are **worried** . . .

Your Father knows the things you need
before you ask Him.
MATTHEW 6:8 ICB

God will meet all your needs.
PHILIPPIANS 4:19 NIV

LIVE YOUR FAITH

Dear Friend,

This book was prayerfully crafted with you, the reader, in mind. Every word, every sentence, every page was thoughtfully written, designed, and packaged to encourage you—right where you are this very moment. At DaySpring, our vision is to see every person experience the life-changing message of God's love. So, as we worked through rough drafts, design changes, edits, and details, we prayed for you to deeply experience His unfailing love, indescribable peace, and pure joy. It is our sincere hope that through these Truth-filled pages your heart will be blessed, knowing that God cares about you—your desires and disappointments, your challenges and dreams.

He knows. He cares. He loves you unconditionally.

BLESSINGS!
THE DAYSPRING BOOK TEAM

———————

Additional copies of this book and
other DaySpring titles can be purchased
at fine retailers everywhere.
Order online at dayspring.com
or
by phone at 1-877-751-4347